MAKING
GEORGIAN & REGENCY COSTUMES
FOR WOMEN

MAKING
GEORGIAN & REGENCY
COSTUMES
FOR WOMEN

Lindsey Holmes

THE CROWOOD PRESS

First published in 2015 by
The Crowood Press Ltd
Ramsbury, Marlborough
Wiltshire SN8 2HR

www.crowood.com

British Library Cataloguing-in-Publication Data
A catalogue record for this book is available from the British Library.

ISBN 978 1 78500 070 6

Dedication
For Geoffrey Herbert Starling, 1926 – 2014
Much missed, granddad, teacher and co-conspirator in many a fanciful costume project,
despite never being able to get a word in edgeways.

Typeset by Sharon Dainton, The Design Co-operative Ltd.
Printed and bound in India by Replika Press Pvt Ltd

Contents

Acknowledgements 7

Introduction

Part 1 11

1 A History of Women's Dress 1710 to 1830 13

2 Tools 27

3 Techniques and Fabrics 31

4 Pattern Alteration and Fit 41

5 Underpinnings and Accessories 51

Part 2

6 Project 1: Early Mantua and Masquerade Costume 67

7 Project 2: *Robe Volante* and Caraco Jacket 75

8 Project 3: *Robe de Cour* 85

9 Project 4: *Robe à la Française* 91

10 Project 5: *Robe à L'Anglaise* and Riding Habit 97

11 Project 6: *Robe à la Polonaise* 105

12 Project 7: *Chemise à la Reine* 109

13 Project 8: Directoire Gown and Circus Costume 113

14 Project 9: Regency Gown and Spencer 119

15 Project 10: Late Regency Gown and Ballet Costume 125

16 Patterns for Underpinnings, Skirts, Petticoats
and Accessories 133

Notes 156

Suppliers 158

Suggested Reading 159

Index 160

Acknowledgements

It takes a lot more than one person to make a project like this a reality. Meet the team that made this book possible.

Photographer: Glyn Reed, Lovelylight images

Glyn's first darkroom was in an unlikely place, being in the corner of a rocket launch control room on board a Royal Navy Leander class frigate. Some years later and after a few photos in *Navy News*, he moved to Kodak. Technical support for large photo processing laboratories and training of photo industry personnel followed. Some photographic gaps and training as a teacher in later life has brought him round full circle. Exhibitions, national broadsheet press, regular pages in *Rowing & Regatta*, commercial work with large companies and lately an exciting project with a four-man crew planning to row across the Atlantic.

Illustrations and Retouching: Stuart Holmes

Aside from being a very talented designer, Stuart also has the great misfortune of being the author's husband. When it is possible to escape from various unpaid jobs for his wife, he works as a landscape architect.

Stylist: Heather McIlroy

Heather has worked in fashion and retail for two decades, covering styling, visual merchandising, window displays, creating garments and homewares, and even recovering furniture upholstery. She has travelled the world, and is passionate about interiors, design, architecture and all things fashion. On the side, Heather also coxes a men's rowing crew.

Hair Designer: Toni Tatlow

Toni began her career in hairdressing at the age of eighteen, and joined P.Kai in 2011. She is passionate about creative hair-ups, and about the art of hair. In 2014 Toni reached the regional finals of the Wella Trend Vision competition, and is also the mother of two small boys.

Hair Salon: P.Kai

P.Kai Hair opened in Hampton, just outside Peterborough, in 2002. The salon owners, Kai and Jenny, opened their smaller city-centre salon in the Victorian Westgate Arcade in 2008. The salons have enjoyed continued growth and success in the Cambridgeshire area and beyond, and have been featured in consumer and trade publications worldwide.

Make-up Artist: Rebecca Jefferson

Rebecca is a freelance make-up artist and hair stylist. She graduated from West Thames College with a BA (Hons) in Specialist Makeup and Hair, which covered areas as far and wide as intricate body paint and avant-garde hair to special effects, bridal and period work. Web: www.rebeccajeffersonmua.com.

Proofreader: Peter Starling

Although Peter is technically retired, he chose to come out of retirement to work exclusively on Lindsey's first book, a fact that has absolutely nothing to do with his being her uncle.

Models

Georgia Delve

Georgia is a professional dancer and model with a fervent passion for historical costume and culture. Her interest in the social protocols of dance lead directly into the fashions of the ballroom, and Georgia enjoys creating period costumes for herself and for friends. She is a regular (fully costumed) attendee at Regency balls and loves to bring her historical dance-based research together with her love of costume.

Alison Dunbar

Alison studied Arabic and Middle East Studies at St Andrews University, and currently works in Glasgow. As well as extensive travel and outdoor pursuits such as hill walking, Alison also enjoys the creative arts of knitting, soapstone carving and pottery. She has a special love for the Regency and Georgian periods and wearing the dresses her great-great-grandmothers would have worn. Alison also dabbles in period millinery and dressmaking.

Left: The team.

Camille Lesforis

Camille is a recent graduate of Central Saint Martins University, where she studied design and practice. She is passionate about creating art installations, writing children's stories and character creation and design. Her love of period dramas and costumes inspires her work, and Camille plans to pursue a career in narrative design, and inspiring the creative skills of children through story writing.

Rachel Parton

Rachel is a costumier with over thirty years of design and making experience in costumes and props. She is a member of a medieval re-enactment group and also volunteers as a Victorian costumed room guide for the National Trust. Rachel also enjoys trying out period recipes and crafts as part of her interest in experimental archaeology.

Kirsten Stoddart

Kirsten is an Australian scriptwriter and musician, and spends her working days in film and television production offices. She is a lover of vintage and historical clothing, culture and knick-knacks, and enjoys creating historically inspired events and projects for work and pleasure. Web: www.kirstenstoddart.com.

Kelly Walpole

Kelly has been passionate about the Georgian period since the age of thirteen, when she watched the television series *Sharpe* with her father. Since then, she has been fascinated by the people, fashions and architecture of the Georgian period, which has inspired a creative path of re-enactment, balls and country dances, and an impressive wardrobe of Georgian costumes spanning from 1750 to 1812.

Bryony Woodgate

Bryony is a professional model and football blogger with a degree in Classics. She lives in London. Although she is happy to model historical clothes for her sister Lindsey, she would rather be watching the football. Web: www.toffeelady.co.uk.

Sebastian

Sebastian is a fifteen-year-old Pomeranian. He has lived in Australia, England and Ireland, and enjoys sleeping, posing, making friends and modelling his winter wardrobe.

An additional thank you to the following people for their hard work:

- Costume Assistants: Jo Sandbach and Rachel Parton
- Runners: Wendy Adamczyk and Laura Clappison
- Props: Edie Curtis, Heather McIlroy, Kelly Walpole and Brenda Capitan
- Fabric: Whitchurch Silk Mill.

I would also like to thank everyone who supported me in creating this book, especially my ever-supportive friends and family.

Korina, Bryony and Kitt model the robe à l'anglaise with front opening bodices.

Introduction

                18 Folgate Street, Dennis Severs[1]

Costume has been my world now for
over ten years, and I make garments
that are as historically accurate as
possible. This includes using
handwoven cloth, hand-stitched seams
and corsets with hand-picked and
dried reeds for boning. I have also had
to ensure that the costumes can be
quick to put on, worn over clothing,
machine-washable and resistant to
being pulled seam from seam by
fighting children.

Clothing is magical; it has the power
to give us a moveable, touchable
glimpse of the past. Like a painting
come to life, costume allows us to peek
inside the frame and explore all life
through dress.

From the first moment I held an
Elizabethan stomacher in my gloved
hands as a student, wide-eyed and
hardly daring to breathe, I knew I
wanted to work with dress. I have had
the opportunity not just to remake
period dress but also to handle and
study original items in museums all
over the UK and abroad.

All of this has been fed into my
teaching practice and led me to write
this book, which has been designed
very much with the user in mind.

How to Use this Book

My aim in writing this book is to create
something both beautiful to look at and
easy to use. I also want you to be able
to make your own costumes by
following instructions and adapting the
patterns to make the designs your own.
This book is divided into two parts. The
first half sets out the context, giving
you all of the information you should
need to decide what to make and how
and where to wear it. However, as it is
impossible to show within this book all
of the changes that have occurred in
fashion over such a large and varied
time frame, there is much more to learn
about this period in history. If you want
to do so, you could always start with the
suggested reading at the end of the
book, which covers many of the sources
that have inspired me.

The second half of the book is a
guide for making ten costumes plus a
range of undergarments and
accessories. I have set out each of these
chapters as projects including a little
history on each design and its use,
together with patterns and instructions
for making them.

Naturally there is a crossover
between the first and second sections.

Textile techniques shown in the first
section are used in practice on
costumes in the second section.
Wherever possible I have signposted
this to help you navigate your way
around the book and find what you
need.

All of the patterns in the book are a
standard UK size 12. Chapter 4 shows
you how to adapt the patterns to fit
different sizes. I have done this for the
models in the book as they are a range
of sizes.

My construction methods are a
mixture of period and modern
techniques. Wherever a modern
process is used, I have tried, if possible,
to give the period method. However,
my main aim was to create projects that
are easy to follow and garments that
look historically accurate for the era.

For five of the designs I have adapted
the patterns to create a different look.
This is to show how simple it is to
create something quite different by
using the same pattern. Each
alternative view is based on a
contemporary image. I hope you will
find images that appeal to you and that
inspire you to develop your own
designs.

PART ONE

Chapter 1 – A History of Women's Dress 1710 to 1830

One has as good be out of the world as out of fashion.

Love's Last Shift, Colley Cibber[1]

The long eighteenth century (1710 to 1830) was a period of great change, both politically and socially. Many aspects of life changed dramatically and all of this change had a direct or indirect effect on the development of fashionable dress. It is just as impossible for me to cover all of the fashion worn in this period as it would be to list all of the key social and political changes. Instead I have tried to cover a few key developments to give you a taste of the eighteenth century, especially those developments that had an impact on women and their wardrobes. Much of the timeline focuses on developments in Britain, France and the Americas, and I have tried where I can to reflect the key people and developments in other countries.

A Life through Dress

Dress is special, as our whole lives can be mapped through what we wear. Clothing marks each stage of our lives, and we are judged on what we choose to wear. Viewers read our development, accomplishments, character, position and even our cleanliness from how we look. In this way we are no different from our eighteenth-century sisters, but unlike us, for many eighteenth-century women, clothes were among the few possessions they owned, and often dress was one of the few things women had any control over. Dress was a rare opportunity for women to express their individuality. This was not restricted to women of means, as cheaper items such as ribbons and handkerchiefs meant fashionable expression was within the grasp of most women.

Kings and Queens

Our timeline covers one queen and four kings. Queen Anne dies after being unable to produce a living heir and the country is left with the uncertainly of a new and unknown royal family. A similar situation is mirrored over a hundred years later when Queen Victoria takes the throne. In fact our timeline very nearly starts and finishes with a female ruler, Queen Victoria coming to the throne just after our timeline finishes. Add to this the additional upheaval of George III's insanity and the resulting Regency period and you have a time of great unease. Changes in the surrounding royal courts of Europe and the colonies were hardly stabilizing.

aspect of their lives that they they could control. But in revolutionary France, what you wore could save you from, or send you to, the dreaded guillotine. While clothes in the streets changed a great deal, court dress, which was the formal clothing worn in the presence of the royal court, changed very little. At the start of the timeline, formal court dress would have appeared the same as the mantua in Project 1, changing to the *robe de cour* in Project 3, then changing to the more informal *robe à la française* until the Revolution took place. British courtiers, however, continued to have to wear the strange and awkward combination of Empire line bodices with pannier skirts up to the 1820s.

An Age of Enlightenment

The excitement of the Enlightenment, and the idea of reforming society by using reason, challenging the existing principles grounded in tradition and faith, and advancing knowledge through science, defines the exciting developments of this time. In many ways the modern world is created before our eyes, in a period that starts with the remnants of the dark ages and progresses towards the world we know today.

The novel as we know it today was created in the eighteenth century, and classic stories such as Daniel Defoe's *Robinson Crusoe* and Jonathan Swift's *Gulliver's Travels* were written. The rococo style grew outwards from Paris in the early eighteenth century and impacted on all aspects of the visual arts. Key features of the look were light colours, asymmetrical designs, curves and lots of gold. This was a reaction against its more formal predecessor, baroque. Rococo itself was overtaken at the end of the eighteenth century by the neoclassical style, which drew heavily from ancient Greece and Rome, and was complemented by similar classical fashions.

In medicine, Edward Jenner's vaccine marked the end of the disfiguring scars of smallpox. In Britain, the annual death rate from

The Wider World

Even though eighteenth-century women looked to France for fashion inspiration, this does not mean that British fashions were the same. Not all French fashions were taken up by British women or those in the colonies, and fancy French dressing was not appreciated by many Brits. French styles put their wearers at risk of being greeted with insults as they walked the streets of London.

However, the people of France had a good deal more than fashion to worry about. At the start of our timeline France was on the cusp of financial ruin, this being due to nearly continuous wars, often with Britain. Later in the century, under King Louis XVI, a growing distance evolved

between the royal family and the people, ending in the French revolution. This was followed by the rise and fall of an ambitious lieutenant colonel named Napoleon. The Americas had a revolutionary war of their own, breaking from the British Empire and declaring their independence with the Treaty of Paris in 1783.

All of this upheaval had a great impact on what people wore. Wars meant imported silks from France and cotton from America became scarcer and more expensive. War has always had an impact on fashion; military detailing and simpler lines were in part a result of the Napoleonic wars. In times of trouble many people sort solace in the details of fashion, as an

Perhaps it was the strict rules of court life that made masquerades so popular in the eighteenth century, spreading across Europe from Italy. The freedom to disguise your identity and dress up as someone else, be it a goddess or a shepherdess, must have provided a welcome break from court life and the perfect excuse for a new gown. Much like today, many costumes of historical figures were adapted to suit the fashionable shapes of the day. To find out more, see Project 1.

Alison walking Sebastian in a polonaise, fashionable in the late 1770s.

smallpox fell during the nineteenth century from about 2,000 per million to under 100 per million. Within our own bodies, new discoveries were being made all the time. In the early years of the nineteenth century, René Laënnec invented the stethoscope and listened to the heart and lungs to help diagnose chest conditions. In 1781 William Herschel discovered a new planet outside the then known world. Some of these discoveries, such as Antoine Lavoisier's and Joseph Priestley's identification of oxygen in 1778, helped us to understand our world a little better. Revelations, such as the rising number of discoveries by fossil hunters, such as Mary Anning, and proof of extinction brought forward by Georges Cuvrer in 1796, increased our knowledge of the past.

When most people think of dress and laws, they think of sumptuary laws. These were designed to restrain luxury or extravagance, limiting who wore certain colours, fabrics or trims as well as other items. Unlike other countries at this time, England did not have any such laws in place. France did, but these were often disregarded and rarely enforced. However, laws did have an impact on what people wore in

England. By the time George I sat on the throne, politicians had more power than kings, and lawmakers had an influence on every aspect of people's lives. Laws can give us an idea of how poorer people lived. Whilst clothing could be a source of great pride, the lack of it could also be a source of great shame. In 1697 the Settlement Act required paupers and their families to wear a capital P on their clothing. Punishment for disobeying this could be the loss of relief, imprisonment, hard labour or whipping. However, given the right push the law could also provide for the poor. The Heath and Morals of Apprentices Act of 1802

applied to cotton mills and required all apprentices to be provided with two suits of clothes a year. Apprentices were unpaid and tied to their employer for a fixed term with no guarantee of a paid job at the end of their tenure, but they were provided with food and board. These were the people who helped the fabric trade to grow.

A Woman's Place

When studying women's fashions of this time, discussion often turns to how impractical they would be to wear and how little you could do in them. This underlines a sad fact of the period that

very little was generally expected of women other than as a courtly display of a man's riches. If you think women in court dress looked little more than ornaments then you would be right, for what is practicality and comfort in the face of a display of a man's wealth and status? Married women were by law the property of their husbands; at a time when few had a choice in whom they could marry, this could be a dangerous lottery with little chance of escape should things turn out for the worst. Most timelines of the eighteenth century are filled with great achievements by men for men. It is much harder to spot the impact women made; however, there were some very clever, brave, creative, fearless and tireless women who also had a major influence, and I would highly recommend that you research some of these. If nothing else, you will learn how hard women have had to fight for their rights and to become something more than just being what was expected of them. You will also discover and appreciate how much their achievements are still overshadowed today.

Fashions

Fashions moved from the great heights of the headdresses, at the start of the period, to the great widths of the panniers, and back to even greater heights of extravagant and decorative wigs, before entering a period of child-like simplicity. These changing shapes were supported by a wide range of padding, boning, frills and flounces, to mention but a few fashionable underpinnings and devices used to create shape and texture.

Despite all these changes, the shape of dresses at the start of the period already contains all of the essential elements of the classic eighteenth-century look. The bodice, overskirt and petticoat continued to be worn in different guises up until dramatic changes occurred at the end of the century. This type of costume was called the open robe, the centre front being open and showing the petticoat. The closed robe, which was worn later in the period, was almost the same but with no opening in the centre front of the skirt. This was the beginning of modern dress.

Our early mantua, the first project in this book, shows British court dress at this time. Shortly after this, large round hoops or panniers, similar to mid-Victorian crinolines, become fashionable in France. Fashion in France at this time was more informal, perhaps because of the Regency when Louis XV came of age in 1723. The large hoops could be worn with the *robe volante* to make it more formal. Once the hoop starts to flatten out, we start to see the beginnings of the new court fashion, born in France but with variations that were worn in many European courts. By 1740 panniers get to their widest and the classic eighteenth-century look is created when panniers are joined by the sack back and flounced lace cuffs. By the 1760s hair begins to rise and hoops are made in two folding pieces, making them much simpler to wear and move in. The Romantic movement in the 1770s, with its emphasis on the simple and natural, was complemented by the fitted and newly closed English gown: the *robe a l'anglaise*, and the *robe à la polonaise* with its looped-up skirt and shorter petticoat. Pads started to replace hoops, and Marie Antoinette's *chemise à la reine* lead the way to the new simple Grecian look at the end of the century. The simple floor-length gowns with long trains, fitted bodice with high waists and short puff sleeves resemble children's dress. By 1815 this

Life in eighteenth-century England was typified by the landed gentry staying at their county manors away from court life and enjoying a simple and practical outdoor lifestyle. Nothing typified this more than the English woollen riding habit. When it became fashionable in France to dress *à l'anglaise*, this was the costume to have. This is perhaps one of the most masculine and practical outfits a lady might have in her wardrobe at this time. To find out more, see Project 5.

Georgia reads in a silk evening gown.

new simple style is established, with shorter and wider skirts, more frills and the Spencer jacket and poke bonnet. As we approach the end of our timeline, the classic Regency look starts to transform into the early Victorian style, and hence our last project shows the lowering waistline, the skirt continuing to widen and the sleeves starting to grow, ready to become the next outlandish fashion. The eighteenth century really was a period of extremes.

Shopping

Although you could now go to a shop and buy fabric and ribbon, go to a mantua-maker and have a dress made for you, or even buy some items off the peg, the process of fabric to fashion was very different to what we know now. Many of the things we take for granted today simply did not exist at this time. There were no sewing machines, every stitch was completed by hand and the women making the stitches had only daylight or candlelight to work by. Labour was cheap and easy to come by, whilst fabric was expensive and precious and the sort of thing you would pass down in your will. Naturally this impacted on how garments were made, with stitches often designed to be easily undone so that the fabric could be reworked into something new.

Fabrics

Perhaps one of the things that most impacted on our theme is the development of fabrics and the increasing mechanization of textile production. This change allows fabric production to leap forward, with it becoming much faster and more detailed and providing a greater choice of materials.

Traditionally, Britain traded in wool and linen. The output of woollen cloth increased dramatically over this period, supported not just by developments in the weaving process but also by the popularly of tailored garments for both men and women, at home and abroad. Linen was the staple cloth for everything, from undergarments to aprons, and hats to stockings, but cotton was soon to rival linen, starting with printed gowns and working though the whole wardrobe. Other fabrics followed, with an influx of

Protestant weavers from France fleeing persecution and creating a unique opportunity and a new industry in silk.

Our timeline covers a period of growth in silk weaving in Britain. This was further boosted by the ban of imported silks in 1773. The fact that silkworms could not be cultivated in Britain kept prices high, and meant that the raw materials still had to be imported. The beauty of the final project could stand in stark contrast to the misery and poverty of its makers as industrial action on hours, pay and a lack of government support occurred. This was a consistent feature throughout the period. However, the industry could offer women new and better-paid jobs, which was something they were quick to take advantage of:

To dress in the greatest extravagance, so much so that on a Sunday those who formerly moved in the most humble social sphere and appeared in woollens and stuffs have lately been so disguised as to be mistaken for persons of distinction.

English Country Life, E. W. Bovill[2]

At the start of our timeline cottons are available but expensive, as they are imported from India. Later, once they start to be woven and printed in Europe, the development of cheaper printing processes made printed cottons available to a wider clientele. Their popularity then increases as their cost drops. By the end of the eighteenth century cotton has stolen silk's crown as the fashionable fabric, and silk weavers are copying popular printed cotton designs. In 1820 the annual average value of cotton exports from Britain was £28,000. This is equivalent to over £1.5 million in today's money. Samples from the vast collection at the Foundling Museum show that even the poorest women had access to colour and prints. Even if they could not afford the fabric for a new dress, ribbons were a cheap and easy way of dressing up an outfit.

Manners and Etiquette

Dress, manner and carriage are just what she wants, a person must be a great beauty to look well without them, but they are certainly within the reach of any body of understanding.

The Letters of Fanny Brawne to Fanny Keats 1820–1824, Fanny Brawne[3]

The correct way to stand with the arms neither forwards nor backwards nor too close to the body.

The correct way to give or to receive.

The meaning of manners and etiquette are not so clear-cut today as they were in the eighteenth century; etiquette is perhaps the concept we come across the least today. Etiquette is a code of behaviour that dictates expectations for social behaviour according to contemporary norms within a society, social class or group. Manners are a person's bearing or way of behaving towards others, and whether the way in which a thing is done is socially acceptable or not.

During the long eighteenth century, knowledge of these standards and behaviours was a symbol that you were a genteel member of the upper classes. Everyone wanted to be accepted and aspired to reach the next step of the social ladder. This developed into an obsession about the precise rules of current etiquette. By the end of our timeline – the start of the Victorian era – etiquette had developed into a complex system of rules, covering everything from the smallest to the largest duties and interactions, that was do deep-rooted it took a world war to break them down.

Every aspect of life was impacted by etiquette and dress was an instant visual sign of this. The art of dressing well was necessary to gain entrance to established society. There are contemporary accounts of female thieves using fashionable dress to gain people's trust. Changes in fashion, both large and small, were a way to ensure the upper classes remained elite. They had in their arsenal the weapon of ridicule to keep outsiders in their place. As silhouettes did not change a great deal for large parts of the eighteenth century, the devil was very much in the smaller details. Everything needed to add up if you were to cut a fashionable figure. Much was written on this subject at the time. Books were published and quickly became outdated. New periodicals meant updates could be given much more frequently, but the very nature of fashion meant this was left open to interpretation. As *The Mirror of Graces* states:

There is nothing, however minute in manners, however insignificant in appearance, that does not demand some portion of attention from a well-bred and highly-polished young women.[4]

The proper behaviour in dancing.

Giving one hand in a minuet.

You may often be seen to smile, but never heard to laugh while you live. Frequent and loud laughter is characteristic of folly and ill manners.[6]

The fashionable shape up until the end of the century was an inverted cone for the bodice. Stays were worn from childhood to help create the right shape. Breasts were pushed up, and a small waist tapered from the mid bust. Shoulders were pushed back. Slim arms and sloping shoulders were considered beautiful. This solid shape was the one that gowns were built on.

Each stage of an eighteenth-century women's day required different clothes. In her memoirs Jeanne Louise Henriette describes how Marie Antoinette chose dresses for the day:

> The valet of the wardrobe on duty presented every morning a large book to the femme de chambre, containing patterns of the gowns, full dresses, undresses etc. Every pattern was marked to show to which it belonged. The first femme de chambre presented this book to the queen on her awakening, with a pincushion; her majesty stuck pins in those articles which she chose for the day – one for the dress, one for the afternoon dress and one for the full evening dress for card or supper parties in the private apartments.[7]

Marie Antoinette chose three dresses for the day, with each change of dress needed for different activities. The main types of dress are discussed below.

Undress

This is the most informal type of dress, also known as morning dress; the modern equivalent would be casual dress. Worn until mid to late afternoon, this was clothing you would be happy to wear for receiving visitors at home, but would not normally be suitable if you left the house. This type of dress would have been designed to be more

Who would risk overlooking something that held so much influence? As fashion herself says in Giacomo Leopardi's dialogue between fashion and death in 1824:

> Obviously you don't seem to know the power of fashion.[5]

Dancing was a very public way of showing how well you could conduct yourself and how gracefully you could move. Your dress needed to be up to the task: too short a petticoat could cause a scandal and a long train could risk embarrassment, if not handled correctly. The first step to dancing well was good posture.

Francis Nivelon's *The Rudiments of Genteel Behaviour*, published in 1737, states that ladies must keep their head erect and their shoulders back, their arms to the elbow must fall gracefully and the hands should be kept crossed.

When it comes to movement, just walking gracefully in hooped dresses could be quite a challenge. They have a tendency to swing and wobble if your steps are too large, and small steps are needed instead to allow you to appear to glide. In court dress, doorways presented their own challenges, as did the custom of never turning your back on the king or queen, which required you to be equally skillful walking forwards and backwards with a train. No wonder so many people took lessons, to avoid embarrassment at best and being shunned at worst. Alongside deportment, facial expressions were also key, for society dictated when and when not to express emotion:

The neoclassical influence on dress gave ballet a boost as it started developing into the art form we would recognize today. Changes in fashion meant dancers could abandon bulky hoops and stiff costumes for floating Grecian style dresses that emphasized the body. These dresses meant the dancers could showcase a greater range of movement. Dancers started to wear flat slippers, which gave them greater flexibility in the foot, and allowed them to develop the trick of rising on tiptoe; this was also the period when the first famous ballet stars came to the fore, women such as Marie Anne de Cupis de Camargo and Marie Taglioni. To find out more, see Project 10.

comfortable and warmer than more formal dress. Of the projects in this book the *robe volante* could have been worn as undress at home by ladies rich enough to afford it. Richer women also would have worn Caraco jackets at home, but working women would have worn these out of the house.

Day dress

Dresses designed to be worn outside during the day had lots of different names: walking dresses, promenade dresses, carriage dresses and later, as visits to spa towns became more popular, seaside dresses. These were all popular topics covered by fashion plates in this period. Another outdoor outfit was the riding costume; later in the century it also came to be known as a travelling costume. Outside activities gave women the chance to show off their clothing and admire those of

others. The *robe à l'anglaise*, the riding habit, the *robe à la polonaise*, the *chemise à la reine* and the Regency gown could all be suitable for this use.

Full dress

This was worn for formal events, parties, balls, concerts and weddings; the modern equivalent would be evening dress. This term was used then, but it was also called night dress. The concept of a dress just for your wedding day was formed in the Victorian era. In the eighteenth century an existing dress would do. It is important to remember throughout this period that evening events would have been lit by candlelight, so it would have been by candlelight that these dresses would have been seen. Contemporary advice asks women to remember this when choosing colours for evening apparel. The difference between day dress and evening dress was more than just fabric, as *The Mirror of the Graces* describes:

> In the morning the arms and bosom must be completely covered to the throat and wrists. From the dinner hour to the termination of the day, the arms to a graceful height above the elbow, may be bare; and the necks and shoulders unveiled as a far as delicacy will allow.[8]

Accessories needed to be as well matched to the dress as the dress was to the activity. Nearly all of the dresses in this book could be full dress in the right fabrics, but the following are good examples: the early mantua, the *robe à la française*, the Directoire gown and the late Regency gown.

Court dress

Also called the grand habit, this was a specific formal type of full dress worn at court and for other formal royal occasions. For much of the period this involved hoops, trains and ostrich feathers worn in the hair, but court fashions varied from court to court. White was not yet the established

colour for a wedding dress, which at this time could be any colour. For court weddings royal brides and grooms wore gold. In England, brides were often presented at court in their wedding dress. Examples of projects that could be court dress are the early mantua, the *robe de cour*, the Directoire gown and the late Regency gown.

Pregnancy and dress

There was no established maternity clothing; most women just adjusted their usual clothing. Clothing with lacing such as the *robe volante* and the *robe à la française* could be let out and stomachers replaced with larger, less stiff pieces of fabric. It was common at this time to tie an apron over the bump just below the bust. Although some women swapped corsets for softer, unboned clothing such as waistcoats, many continued to wear them. Pregnancy stays with side laces, which could be adjusted as you grew, have survived. The Empire line was much more convenient for accommodating a bump, as can be seen in the Directoire gown and the Regency gown.

The new freedom from heavy costume, which enabled ballet to progress at the end of the century, also benefited other female performers. Contemporary illustrations show female circus artists performing tricks such as rope-walking and balancing acts in short Empire line gowns. Skills such as these must have been much less hazardous and more visually impressive in shorter skirts. To find out more, see Project 8.

1708 The first semi-public masked ball is held at the Haymarket Opera House in London.

1710 St Paul's Cathedral in London is completed.

1710 Jacob Christoph Le Blon develops a three-colour paper printing process.

1711 The composer George Frideric Handel first visits London.

1714 Queen Anne dies; George I becomes King.

1717 Handel is commissioned to write music for a royal water party, and composes *The Water Music* to accompany King George I's progress along the River Thames.

1718 Lady Mary Wortley has her daughter successfully inoculated for smallpox in Turkey and begins campaigning for inoculation in Britain.

Early mantua silhouette 1715.

1719 Weavers lead protest attacks on women wearing calicoes in Spitalfields, London.

1720 The South Sea Company collapses, creating the South Sea Bubble financial scandal.

1721 A regular postal service is introduced between London and New York.

1721 Jane Wenham from Hertford is the last woman convicted for witchcraft in England.

1722 Giuseppa Barbapiccola writes in her preface to her translation of René Descartes *Principles of Philosophy*: 'But then if one looks carefully and clearly, women should not be excluded from the study of the sciences, since their spirits are more elevated and they are not inferior to men in terms of the greatest virtues.'[9]

1722 Daniel Defoe's *Moll Flanders* is published.

1726 Jonathan Swift's *Gulliver's Travels* is published.

1727 King George II is crowned.

Robe volante silhouette 1730.

1730 Britain becomes the largest slave trading country in the world.

1731 Number 10 Downing Street is built in London.

1732 Hogarth begins subscriptions for *A Harlot's Progress,* a series of prints showing a woman's descent into prostitution.

1732 The original Theatre Royal opens in Covent Garden, London.

1733 Elizabeth Canning, an English maidservant, disappears for a month, claiming on her return she has been kidnapped. This becomes one of the most famous English criminal cases of the century.

1733 John Key invents the flying shuttle, allowing a single weaver to weave much wider fabrics.

1736 The gin riots are held in London over The Gin Act, which imposed high taxes on retailers.

1737 François Nivelon's *The Rudiments of Genteel Behavior* is published.

1738 The Tiverton Riot is held in Devon by wool trade workers over the undercutting of prices.

1740 'Rule Britannia' is written by James Thomson and set to music by Thomas Arne.

1741 The first children are admitted to the Foundling Hospital in London. At this time over 75 per cent of children born in London died before they were five.

Robe de cour silhouette 1740.

1742 London's first bathhouse, which also offered a swimming pool, opens.

1744 Eliza Lucas proves that indigo, needed for dye, could be successfully grown and processed in South Carolina.

1744 Eliza Haywood publishes the first issue of *The Female Spectator,* a periodical written by women, for women.

1745 The commercial growing of indigo for dye starts in England.

1745 The term 'middle class' is first used.

1748 Mathematician Maria Gaetana Agnesi's book on *Instituzioni analitiche ad uso della gioventù italiana (Analytical Institutions for the Use of Italian Youth)* is published in Milan.

1751   Copper plate printing, used on fabric, is invented in England.

1752   The Gregorian calendar is introduced, which omitted 3 September to 13 September to correct the 11-day difference. Riots commenced in London over the perceived loss of days.

1752   Benjamin Franklin flies a kite during a thunderstorm in Philadelphia to prove that lightning is electricity.

1753   The British Museum is founded in London and subsequently opened to the public in 1759.

1755   Jean-Jacques Rousseau writes *Discourse on the Origin of Inequality*, in which he denounces private property as the root of all evil.

1756   The Seven Years War begins when Britain declares war on France over trade and colonies.

1759   Harris's list of Covent Garden ladies, an annual directory of London prostitutes, is first published.

Robe à la française
silhouette 1755.

1760   King George III is crowned.

1761   George III buys Buckingham Palace for Queen Charlotte.

1763   Machine-breaking in protest by Spitalfields weavers takes place.

1764   Mozart, aged eight, arrives in London for a stay of over a year as part of a world tour.

1764   Lancelot 'Capability' Brown is appointed chief gardener at the Royal Palace of Hampton Court.

1765   The campaign by Spitalfields weavers against the import of French silks is successful.

1768   Angelica Kauffmann and Mary Moser are the only two women among the 36 founding members of the Royal Academy of Arts.

1768   Phillip Astley stages the first modern circus with acrobats and equestrian stunt riders.

1770   The anatomist Marie Marguerite Bihéron presents her very detailed and lifelike wax model of a pregnant woman, complete with moveable parts and foetuses, to the Academie Royale des Sciences in Paris.

1770   The spinning jenny is patented by James Hargreaves; it reduces the amount of work needed to spin yarn.

1773   The Spitalfields Weavers Act to regulate wages and ban imported silks is passed.

1774   Phillis Wheatley's *Poems on Various Subjects, Religious and Moral* is published; she is the first published African-American woman.

1774   The Royal Crescent in Bath is completed.

Robe à l'anglaise
silhouette 1770.

1776   Riots in Shepton Mallet over the introduction of new machinery in the woollen industry.

1776   The American colonies proclaim their independence.

1778   Antoine Lavoisier and Joseph Priestley discover oxygen.

1781   French artist Anne Vallayer-Coster is given space to exhibit in the Musée du Louvre following the patronage of Queen Marie Antoinette of France.

1782   Deborah Sampson, dressed as a man, enlists and fights in the revolutionary war in America.

Robe à la polonaise
silhouette 1780.

1782   The Royal Circus opens in the London Hippodrome and the Amphithéâtre Anglais; the first purpose-built circus in Paris is established.

1783   Astronomer Caroline Herschel, sister of William, updates and corrects Flamsteed's work detailing the position of the stars.

1784   French writer Olympe de Gouges writes the anti-slavery play *Zamore and Mirza*.

1786   Henley Bridge is built; it holds two sculptures, Isis and Tamesis, by sculptor Anne Seymour Damer.

1789   The women's march on Versailles is started among women in the marketplaces of Paris over the high price of bread.

1789   Rachel Wall, America's only known female pirate, is executed for robbery and murder in Boston, Massachusetts.

1791   Olmype de Gouges writes *Déclaration des droits de la Femme et de la Citoyenne* (Declaration of the Rights of Woman and the Female Citizen): 'A woman has the right to mount the scaffold; she must equally have the right to mount the rostrum.'[10]

1792   Mary Wollstonecraft writes *A Vindication of the Rights of Woman.*

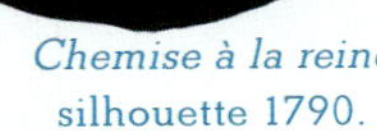

Chemise à la reine silhouette 1790.

1792   Louis XVI of France is arrested and taken into custody, along with his family.

1792   Gustav III of Sweden is shot and killed at a masked ball.

1793   Citizen Louis Capet (formerly known as Louis XVI) is guillotined. Later in the year Marie Antoinette is also guillotined.

1794   Gallery of Fashion, the first fashion magazine, is published.

1796   Edward Jenner creates a successful vaccine for smallpox.

1799   The Association of Lancashire Weavers is formed.

1800   The US capital is established permanently in Washington DC.

1801   The Union Jack is adopted as the flag of Britain.

1802   The Health and Morals of Apprentices Act for cotton mill workers, including instructions that all workers are to have two suits of clothes a year and daily instruction, is passed.

1805   The Battle of Trafalgar is fought by the Royal Navy against the combined fleets of the French and Spanish Navies. A decisive victory is lead by Admiral Lord Nelson.

Directoire style gown silhouette 1800.

1806   Patrick Clark develops a cotton thread as strong as linen.

1807   The Transatlantic Slave Trade is abolished by the British Parliament, although the Abolition of Slavery Act does not come into place until 1834.

1808   Excavations at Pompeii begin.

1809   Mary Dixon Kiesirst is the recipient of the first patent granted to a woman by the United States Patent and Trademark Office, on 5 May 1809, for a technique of weaving straw with silk and thread. Her technique proved valuable in making cost-effective work bonnets.

1811   Jane Austen's first novel *Sense and Sensibility* is published.

1811   The Regency begins, following George III's insanity.

1811   Mary Anning and her brother Joseph discover the fossilized remains of an ichthyosaur at Lyme Regis.

1814   The first powered weaving looms are used in the US.

1814   Napoleon abdicates and is exiled to Elba.

1818   Disturbances are reported during the strike of Manchester cotton spinners.

1820   The battle of Bonnymuir near Glasgow pits weavers against troops.

1820   King George IV is crowned; the Regency ends.

1822   The Rosetta stone is deciphered by Champollion.

1823   The Anti-Slavery Society is formed.

1823   A rubberized cotton is developed by Macintosh.

Regency dress and Spencer silhouette 1815.

1825   Marie-Louise Lachapelle, a French midwife, completes her book *Pratique des accouchements; ou mémoires et observations choisies, sur les points les plus importants de l'art* (The practice of deliveries; or chosen observations and memories on the most important points of the art), which is published posthumously by her niece.

1826/1827   The oldest surviving permanent photograph of the image formed in a camera is created by Niépce.

1829   The first practical sewing machine is invented by Barthélemy Thimonnier, a French tailor.

1833   The abolition of slavery throughout the British Empire.

Late Regency gown silhouette 1825.

1837   Queen Victoria is crowned.

Mourning dress

Mourning dress was a way of showing those around you that you had lost someone. What you wore changed based on how close the person you had lost was to you and the stage of your mourning, deep mouring being all black and half mourning introducing grey or white. Black crepe was a popular fabric for mourning clothing. Women's mourning cothing was a complex issue and more extreme then men's mourning clothing.

The Styles in this Book

You will find more information about each style of dress at the start of each project. The date for each style has been established by looking at surviving garments from the period. However, most of the styles were worn at both earlier and later dates, often overlapping with each other depending on where and when they were worn. Whenever possible, I have tried to give advice on this aspect.

Before you make a costume, think about when it will be worn and the most suitable fabrics to make it in. Researching contemporary fashion plates is a simple way of checking details such as hem lengths and that textile decorations are suitable. Spending a bit of time practising walking and any other required movements can help to avoid accidents. Remember to allow time to make practical adjustments as needed.

CLARK & Cos
BUTTON THREAD
50 YDS.
EXTRA STRONG

Chapter 2 - **Tools**

Byron, Don Juan[1]

As the saying goes, a workman is only as good as his tools. I grew up in a family in which everything could be fixed, improved or made, if the right tools were to hand. Over the years I have collected tools covering every possible job. If you are new to sewing, getting the right tools can be an expensive business, so in this chapter I will cover the essential tools you need to make these costumes and some 'nice to have' items you can add to your wish list.

Sewing Machine

One of the first things you will see when you enter a costume maker's studio is at least one sewing machine. For theatre and film the rule is often that only the stitching that will be seen will be hand-stitched. Re-enactors, however, often take pride in stitching everything by hand for a truly period feel. While you can make any of the items in this book entirely by hand should you wish to, a sewing machine is a very useful item to have, and if used correctly will save you time while still creating a period look. Getting a sewing machine need not be expensive, although many of the cheaper-end new sewing machines are not up to the job of sewing through anything other than the lightest fabric. Most of the costumes in this book were made on my Nana's 1970s Jones, which has turned out endless costumes without complaint. If you can source them, reconditioned older machines

are good value. If not, look for a machine with metal parts and a good warrantee. Remember – sewing machines are like cars; you need to get them regularly serviced, at least once a year if you use your machine weekly. Also you need to learn basic maintenance, oiling, cleaning out of dust, changing bulbs, needles and feet. If you are given a second-hand machine, I suggest having it serviced before you use it.

Needles

You will need suitable needles (sewing machine or hand) for your fabric, for example leather needles for all skins and super sharp microtex needles for silks. When sewing with delicate fabrics it pays to change your needle more often to avoid costly pulls. Always remember to change your needle when you change your fabric!

Thread

Most costume designers still use cotton or silk thread. This is so that costumes can later be dyed and reused without contrasting polyester thread stitching showing up. Unless you have professional dyeing skills or you are willing to pay for them, I would suggest using polyester thread in a colour to match your fabric. This is both cheaper and easier to source. It is also easier to handle, especially if that's what you are used to.

Mannequin

A mannequin (or dressmaker's dummy or dress form) is very useful, especially if you work alone or are making things for yourself. It doesn't matter what type

you have. Ideally, I would suggest getting a smaller one than you need and padding it out to the correct size using wadding. This also allows you to fit corsetry on it and get a similar reaction to a real body. In industry when making lots of different costumes for different people, makers sandwich the wadding between layers of jersey fabric, stitch it all together and have pull-on and off body forms for different people. New dress forms can be expensive, but they can be picked up cheaply second-hand.

Scissors

You will need a pair of paper scissors and a pair of fabric scissors. Never use your fabric scissors for cutting anything other than fabric as this will blunt the blades and fray/pull the fabric. You should also have a small pair of snips for cutting thread. I keep mine on a ribbon around my neck while working, so they are always to hand, although you need to remember to take them off when you are finished to avoid an accident. Your fabric shears should be the right size for your hands. Having

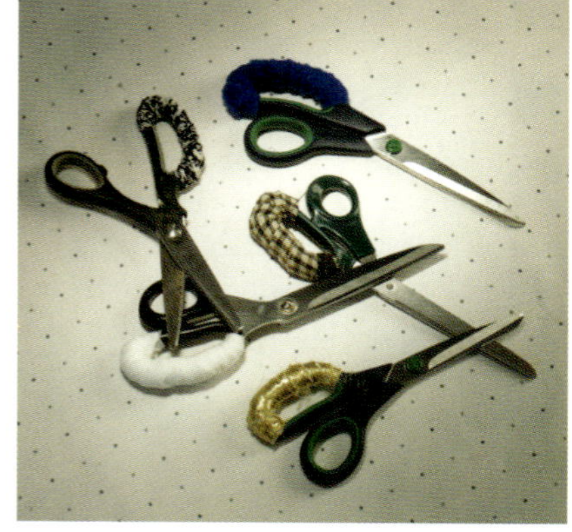

Scissors with fabric-wrapped handles.

Left: Long pins and vintage cotton threads.

the wrong size scissors can lead to injuries. You should be able to open the shears as wide as they will go whilst cutting. If you can't do this, they are too big. Hard-handled shears should be wrapped – I find stretch bandage strapping best, although strips of fabric can also be used.

Stitch Unpick

This is a tool for ripping out stitches, and is useful for adjusting toiles and undoing mistakes.

Weights

Pattern weights can be useful for holding fabric pattern pieces in place, especially if the fabric is very slippery or would show pin marks. You don't have to buy proper pattern weights; anything heavy and clean will do.

Pattern Paper

I use dot and cross paper, which is marked in square inches, but any paper will do. Brown paper works well. Just remember if you use printed paper to check that the ink won't transfer to your fabric.

Masking Tape

This can be drawn on and ironed, unlike plastic tape, so is perfect for patterns.

Measures

You need a tape measure and a length of cotton tape to mark waists while measuring or fitting. A set square is helpful for pattern-cutting, but a large clear flat ruler will do. I also find a metre ruler helpful for measuring larger pattern pieces and fabric.

Pencils

It's best to use harder pencils (HB and H grades) that won't smudge and mark or tailor's chalk. Pencils with an eraser on the end are handy.

Calculator

This is useful to save time when scaling up and adjusting pattern sizes.

Leather Punch

This is useful for making eyelet holes and essential if you plan to work with leather.

Eyelet Punch

If you plan to 'cheat' and use metal eyelets on underwear, an eyelet punch will save time and keep your finished eyelets neat and flat.

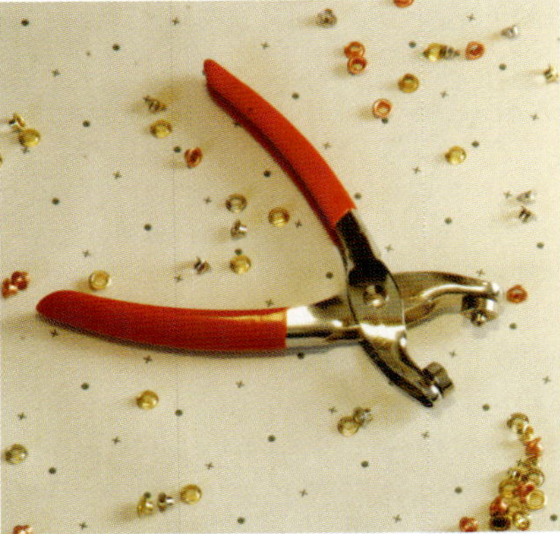

Eyeleter and metal eyelets: quicker to make and stronger to use than hand stitched eyelets, but not period.

Iron and Ironing Board

Keep your iron and board cover clean and always double-check the settings on your iron before pressing your fabric. The first time you iron any fabric, test the iron on a scrap first, and for fine fabrics use a pressing cloth: an old-style cotton handkerchief is perfect for protecting your fabric. A tailor's ham and sleeve press are also useful for corners and fiddly bits, but you can make do with the corners of your ironing board. A steamer is a wish list item useful for awkward shapes and heavy costumes.

Hat Block or Hat Stand

If you plan to make hats or bonnets, a hat block or stand are useful. Keep an eye out for these as they can be found second-hand.

Rouleau Loop Turner

This is useful if you plan to make your own ribbons or trimmings.

Flexi Curve/French Curves

These are useful for adjusting patterns and great if you are not confident at drawing curves freehand.

Safety Pins

These are always useful for fittings and last-minute adjustments. If you plan to secure your dresses the traditional way, using safety pins rather than straight pins will decrease the chances of you accidently drawing blood – yours or another's! With a little practice you can make them look the same as straight pins.

Hooks and Eyes

These were in use in the eighteenth century, but rarely used over pins. However, they offer quite a few advantages to a modern wearer/maker.

Poppers/Snaps/Hook and Loop Tape

These are a much more modern invention, but they offer a quick way of changing if needed. I tend to avoid hook and loop tape (e.g. Velcro) on anything other than rip-off costumes, as the hooks can damage delicate fabrics.

Thimble

If you have a good deal of hand sewing to do, it is worth spending the time to get used to using a thimble, to save your poor fingers. If like me you dislike using them, try sticking plasters.

Pins

As with needles, there are different types of pins for different uses. I prefer bobble-headed pins, as these are easier to handle and spot if they go walkabout. Never put pins in your mouth: you do not want to swallow one and you need to keep them dry and clean.

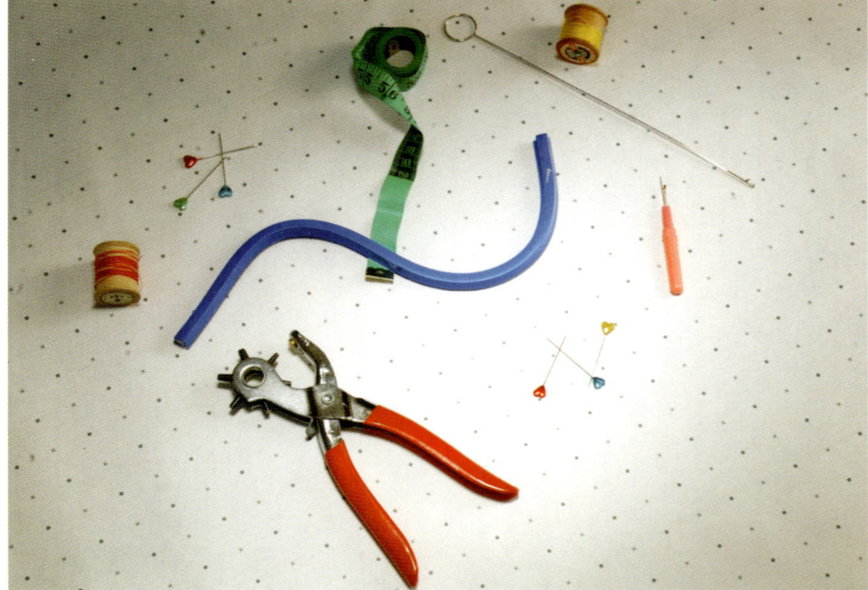

From top left round, tape measure, rouleau loop turner, stitch unpick, leather punch and French curve on dot and cross pattern paper.

Pincushion

Magnetic pin holders are great at ensuring you have picked up any stray pins. For fittings, pincushions that strap on to your wrist are handy.

Workspace

Your workspace is as important as your tools. Even if you don't have a dedicated space, you need to think about the following points in the space you use.

If at all possible, try to avoid using the floor for pattern and fabric cutting. It makes it much harder to keep fabric clean and will damage your knees. If you have no choice, invest in a gardener's kneeling pad. Ideally, if you sew a lot, you would have a dedicated pattern-cutting table, at waist height so you are not bending over too much. If you have a multi-use table, always clean it before you start and clean away anything that could get marked when you finish, especially if you have a partner, like mine, who likes to disassemble engines in the house without warning.

Make sure your work area is well lit, and that you are never doing close work in poor light. If you need to add some desk lights, clip-on or stick-on lights also work well in small spaces.

You also need to think about storage. During construction and after you have made your costumes, make sure you store them well. While making costumes, I have two large plastic tubs, one for 'to sew' pieces and one for 'sewn' pieces. Any currently unused pattern pieces are kept in clear, resealable bags (e.g. ziplock) in another tub of ongoing projects. Delicate hats are best stored in boxes or in inflated clear plastic bags. Never store anything on top of hats. Jars are useful for small items such as snaps, hooks and pins, and clear jars save time in identifying types of fastenings stored in them. A sewing box is sweet, but I have never found one large enough to be useful, although you do need somewhere to keep sharps such as scissors, pins and stitch unpicks. If you can't hang up your items to store them, fold them and put them in garment boxes. And label everything! That way, as you make more items, you can find what you need. There were no such things as hangers or wardrobes in the eighteenth century and many items in this book don't hang well on hangers, unless you add extra ribbon loops secured at the waist that are long enough to reach up to the shoulders and can be looped over a coat-hanger. This distributes the weight of the hanging garment equally, and it is supported from one of the most stable parts of the garment – the waistband.

When starting out, sewing can feel like a dauntingly expensive hobby; but it is possible to sew on a budget. Hand-me-downs from older generations, sharing with sewing friends, and keeping an eye on second-hand outlets and the sales can all help. Once you have tools, take good care of them, and if they are of good quality they should last you a lifetime.

Chapter 3 – Techniques and Fabrics

Sewing Techniques

Basic Hand Stitches

These simple hand stitches are the foundation from which costumes are built; they cover nearly every aspect of construction and with a little practice are simple to perfect.

BACKSTITCH
Much like a period dance, backstitch is created by taking two steps forward then one step back. This is the hand equivalent of the two-thread lock stitch a sewing machine produces and it is a good stitch for holding two pieces of fabric together firmly.

RUNNING STITCH
Much quicker to produce than backstitch, this is good for tacking fabric together to check the fit before machining. It is also the base for the modern gather, by knotting one end

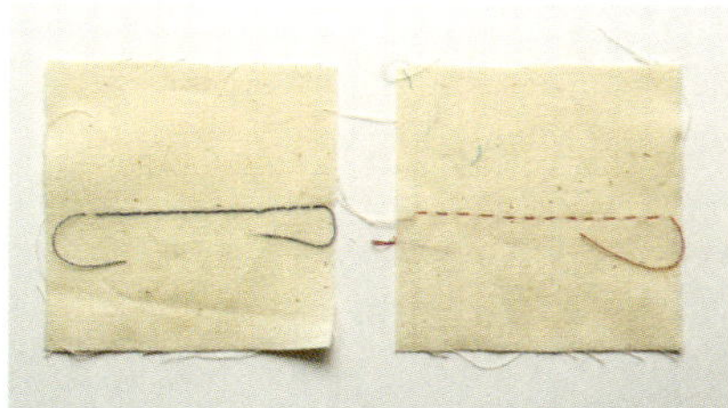

Backstitch and running stitch.

and drawing up the threads, thereby gathering the fabric. This stitch is created by evenly passing the needle in and out of the fabric as shown.

SLIP STITCH
Commonly used for finishing edges or hems, the tension of the thread is much looser here than with other stitches. This stitch is created by catching in turn the folded hem and then the fabric just above the hem, as shown. Your aim in catching up just a few threads of your fabric is for the stitches not to show through on the face side of your fabric, even if stitched in a contrasting thread.

Slip stitch showing back and face sides.

WHIP STITCH
This is used for finishing edges or joining two pieces of fabric together. It is ideal for joining fabrics that won't fray, such as felt or leather, or for joining knitted items. It is also used for finishing the edges of very light fabrics such as silk, chiffon or organza.

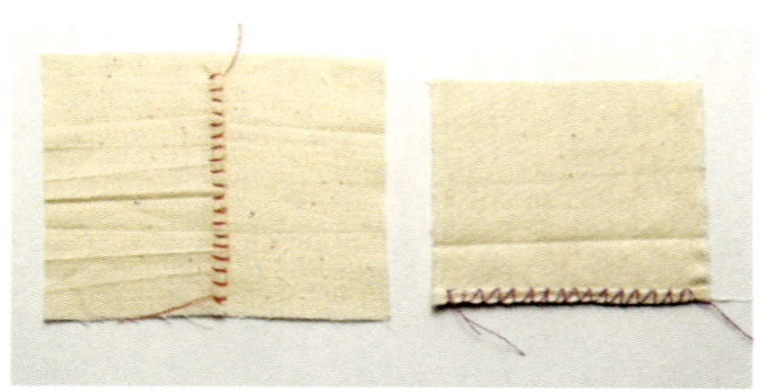

Whip stitch shown as both a hemming and joining stitch.

EYELETS
Hand-stitched eyelets can be made using the buttonhole stitch. This stitch catches a loop of the thread on the surface of the fabric before the needle is returned to the back of the fabric at a right angle to the original start of the thread. To keep the strength of your fabric while making eyelets, it is best not to cut the threads while creating a hole. Instead, create a hole by poking a hole through the centre of the location of your eyelet and gently pushing the threads outwards until you have a suitably sized gap.

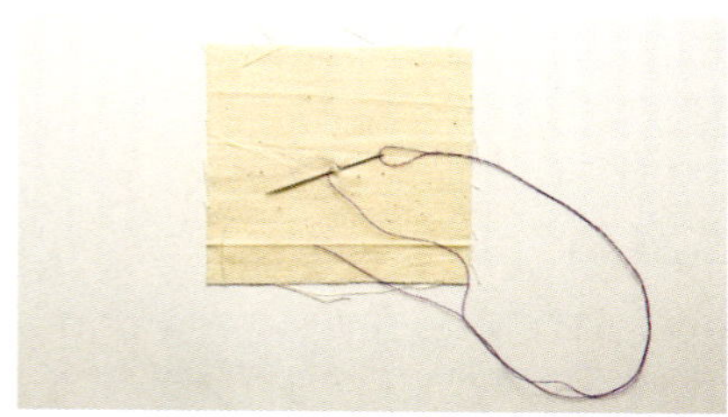

The beginnings of an eyelet.

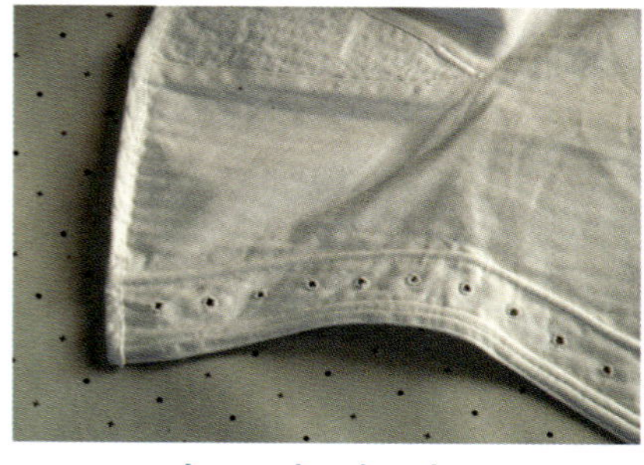

A completed eyelet.

Bust Gores

These are used in the front of short stays to allow more fullness for the bust. Start by pinning and tacking your gore triangles into the slit. Next, try this against your bust to establish what adjustments are needed. If you are not lining your stays, you will need to turn under the seam allowance of the gore

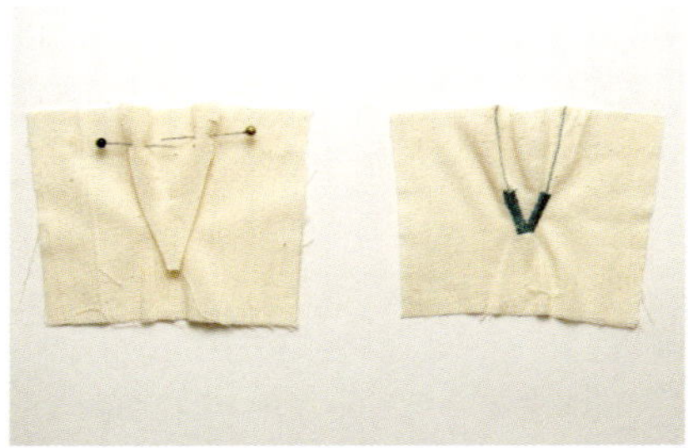

Bust gores, shown in stages.

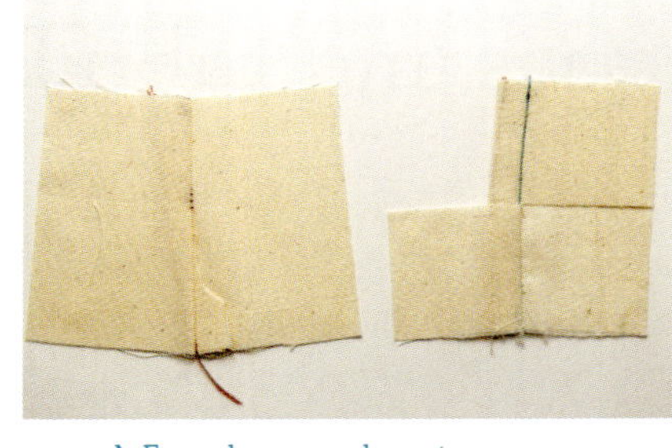

A French seam show in stages.

Felled seam, shown in stages.

and the slits twice, tapering it down to the points. If you are lining the gores, you need only press the seam allowance of the slits inwards. Sew the gore from the top down to about 2.5cm from the bottom of the V using either straight machine stitch or backstitch, then zigzag or overstitch the seam until you reach the same point on the way back up, before returning to straight machine stitch or backstitch to finish sewing the seam.

Seams

In most cases, you can choose how to finish your seams. The following are a range of seams and seam finishes, both period and modern. The basic seam itself is sewn using either backstitch if sewing by hand or straight stitch if using on a machine. The difference is the method with which the raw edges have been finished. All of these seams can be completed by hand or machine.

TURNED AND STITCHED SEAM

This is a modern seam, in which the raw edge is pressed under and then overstitched down with a running stitch or backstitch.

FRENCH SEAM

This is a modern seam, in which the seam is turned over, pressed and then the raw edge is trapped by another line of stitching. When creating this seam you need to remember to start with the wrong sides of the fabric together, rather than right sides together as you would for all of the other seams. With wrong sides of the fabric together, sew a seam that is narrower than the seam allowance. Then trim the allowance, fold the fabric right sides together and press along the stitching line. Now sew a second seam along the intended seam line, enclosing the raw edges of the seam allowance.

OVERCAST SEAM

This can be made by hand or machine. I have seen this stitch used on garments from this period, where the raw edge has been hand-finished with a whip stitch. By using a machine you can zigzag or overlock the raw edge to create the same effect.

FELLED SEAM

This is used for strength and is commonly used in corsetry. This technique was used in the eighteenth

century. Sew the seam, then trim one side of the seam allowance. Turn under or finish the edge of the untrimmed seam allowance, press it over the trimmed seam allowance and stitch down.

BOUND SEAM

This is an eighteenth-century technique, where the raw edges are bound with tape. Bias-cut tape is the easiest to handle, but was not available in the eighteenth century. Using straight-cut tape is more bulky and fiddly, however.

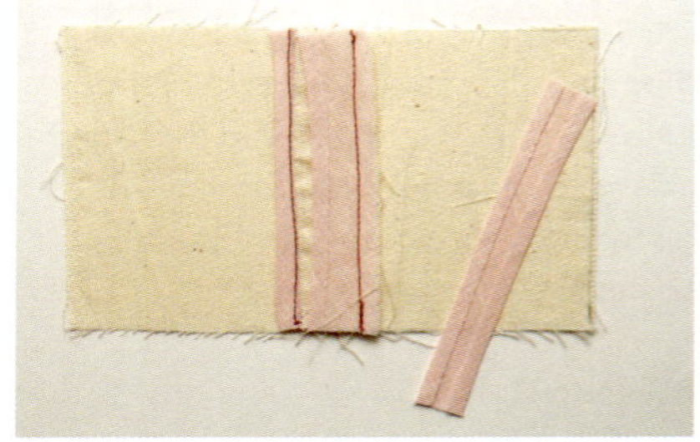

Bound seam, shown in stages.

Lining

If you fully line your garment, you don't need to finish the seam edges, as they won't be handled once they are stitched in and they won't fray to the same extent as open seams. However, if your fabric frays a great deal, you may wish to finish the edges to stop it fraying while you are making it.

Leather

Skin does not fray, but it also cannot be pressed flat with an iron. Seams in leather can be felled, which will keep

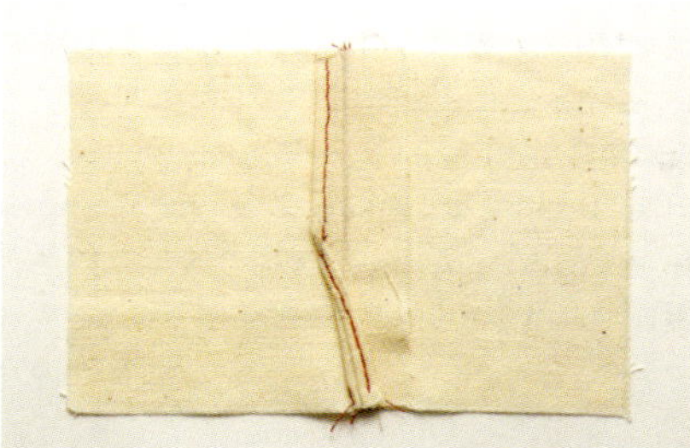

A turned and stitched seam.

Overcast seams finished on a standard sewing machine and an overlocker.

them flat, or if you do not want to fell your seams, you can use a little glue to hold them flat.

Pleats, Tucks and Gathers

Pleats were used to accommodate fullness in the same way that we use gathers today. For small amounts of ease, for example in an armhole, pin tucks are more period than modern gathers, but a little bit more fiddly to create.

PIN TUCKS

Using pins, even out the fullness of the fabric over the gap you need to fit it in to, then continue to pin it in until it is evenly set between each pin. Then hand-stitch in place. Do not put the fabric through the machine with this many pins in, as you are likely to break your needle.

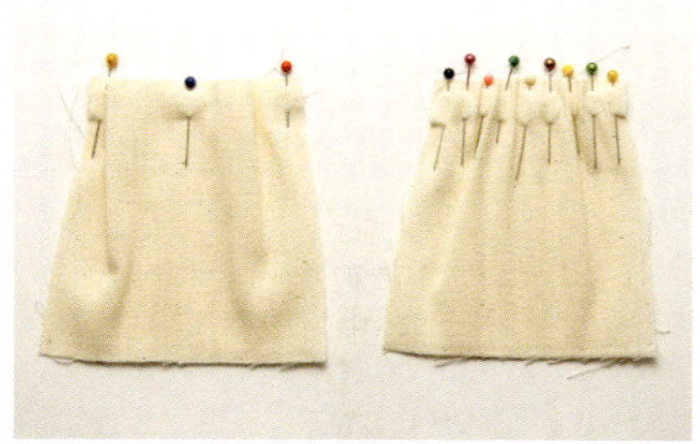

Pin tucks, used to spread fullness.

KNIFE PLEATS

These are a simple pleat that produces a smooth line without being bulky. To create a standard knife pleat, you need to allow a 3 to 1 ratio: that is, three centimetres of fabric to make one centimetre of finished pleat. Should you wish to fit more fabric into your

Knife pleats.

waistband, you can overlap the pleats to accommodate a larger amount of fabric.

BOX PLEATS

These are the foundation of sack back gowns such as the *robe volante* and the *robe à la française* and are simply two knife pleats mirroring each other. An inverted box pleat is the reverse side of a box pleat. Box pleats are often set wider than knife pleats, but the ratio of fabric to pleat remains 3 to 1. Box pleats have more fullness to them than knife pleats and they tend to puff out more. This is something that the fashions of the time made a feature of. To keep pleats in place, you can stay them by stitching them down. This can also ensure the fullness only starts to puff out where you want it to. If you are unsure of the effect you want, test this on your toile before stitching permanently.

Box pleats, showing both sides and stayed pleats.

Reducing Bulk

When sewing corners and curves, using the right techniques can help you ensure your seams lie flat and allow the garment to fit snugly where it needs to.

CORNERS

When turning corners for items such as collars, mitreing the corners allows you to create a sharper point, especially with heavier fabric. After stitching the corner, trim across the top and then down the sides of the seam allowances before turning. You can use a pair of scissors to carefully poke out the corner before pressing.

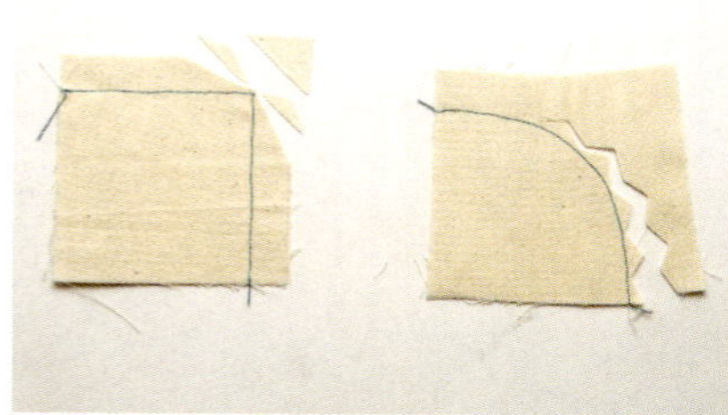

Mitreing corners and trimming curves.

CURVES

The same principle applies to stitching curves. For example on a bodice, reducing the bulk gives you a smoother, flatter shape. To make two different curves meet, it is best to start by pinning them together, matching the ends and notches and easing the fabric in before tacking. Once the curve is stitched, before trimming the seam allowances along the curve as shown, make sure that it will lie flat.

Pinking – the act of cutting the edge of fabric into zigzags or other shapes – was popular during the eighteenth century. This was especially so in the mid to late eighteenth century when used on the edges of the many ruffles that adorned gowns. Pinking shears, now used for stopping the edges of fabrics from fraying and other more decorative uses, were not yet invented. Eighteenth-century pinked edges were made by using metal presses, which stamped the shapes into the edge of silks. However, modern pinking shears can be used.

A ruffle is a strip of fabric, lace or ribbon tightly gathered or pleated along the top edge. These were applied to gowns and other items as a decorative trim, and are simple to make using a running stitch or pleats, as shown. A running stitch can be made straight or zig-zagged to create different effects.

You can use pinking shears to finish the edge of your ruffles. Stitching these to your creations can give a very period look. A running stitch can be made straight or zig-zagged to create different effects.

A flounce is like a ruffle but with less bulk. The difference between the two is in how they are cut. Flounces are cut on

A basket of ribbons and trimmings.

Textile Techniques

> She has ... been all this morning up to the elbows in soap-suds, starch and blue, then on her knees for an hour ironing on the floor.
>
> *Emily Eden on Lady Lansdowne*[2]

Many costumes of the period, both plain and patterned, were further enhanced with textile techniques, often combining different techniques on the same garment. Plain fabrics are normally cheaper than patterned, and decorations are a good way of adding detail without increasing the cost a great deal.

Although it was unusual for rich women, such as Lady Lansdowne, to make or in her case dye fabric for their own clothes, most women decorated fabric or clothing either to wear, to frame or to give as gifts. They faced the same challenges as we do today, with the time spent being a key issue, to ensure completing the fashionable decoration while it was still in fashion. As Maria Josepha Holroyd, working herself a gown in spots in 1790, said:

> I hope the fashions will have the complaisance to wait for me; and that spotted muslins will not go out.[3]

Shown here are some simple and quick but effective techniques that are easy to master and that can be used in a number of ways on a range of garments across our time period. The following is really just a starting point as there are many other techniques and lots of fine examples in museum collections, many of which are online should you wish to research this in more depth.

Whichever techniques you choose, remember to allow extra time to test and complete them. They are easiest to work on flat panel pieces before the garments are made up, but this can be a challenge when working to a deadline!

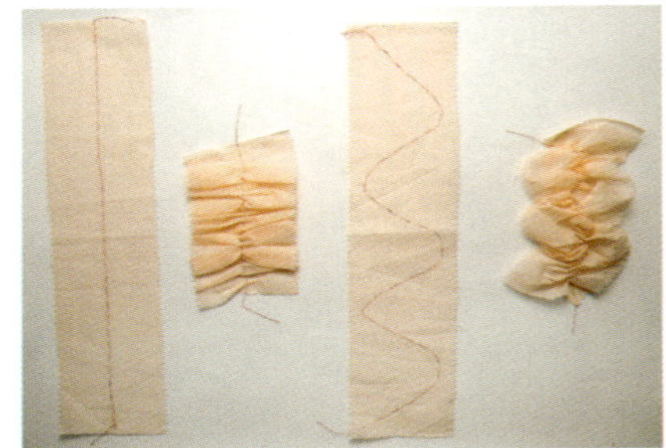

Ruffles, shown in stages.

Ruffles, shown gathered and pleated.

the curve and then straightened to create waves without gathering. The depth of the curve and the width of the fabric determine the amount of wave in the flounce.

Sequins

Sequins have a long history well back into ancient times. Today's sequins are punched from sheets of plastic. Both flat and textured sequins are common. In the eighteenth century they were made from metal, and were most commonly smooth. They are simple to apply by hand if you have a little time and can add a little period sparkle to a gown. The photograph below shows examples of sequins stitched individually and secured with three stitches, and sequins stitched in a chain. Look at period examples for more complex designs; it is best to trace your designs onto your fabric with chalk before you start.

How to stitch sequins.

Aerophane

This is a type of ribbon embroidery that is quite simple to do and can look very effective with a little practice. Strips of crisp silk are woven to create a 3D effect, which was normally a flower.

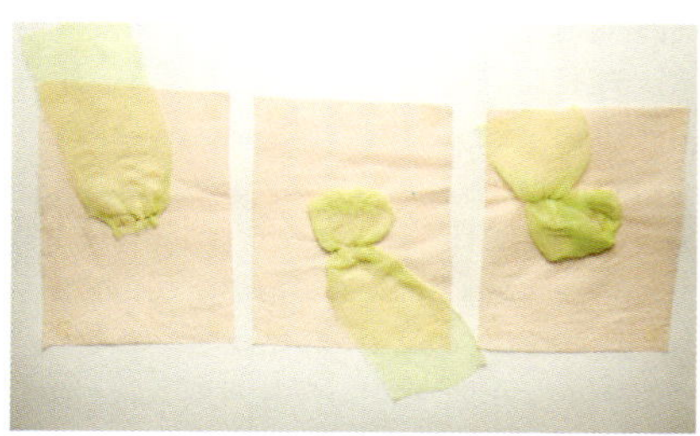

Creating aerophane, in stages.

A completed aerophane flower.

This was very fashionable in the late Regency and early Victorian period. Although it was used before this time, it was most fashionable from the 1830s through to the 1850s.

Bouillonne

Bouillonne (French for bubbles) refers to the fashion fabric puffs commonly shown on eighteenth-century gowns. They are simple to make and are perfect for using up offcuts of fabric and to add texture and detail to grander designs. They are often shown down the fronts of open court gowns like the one in Project 4.

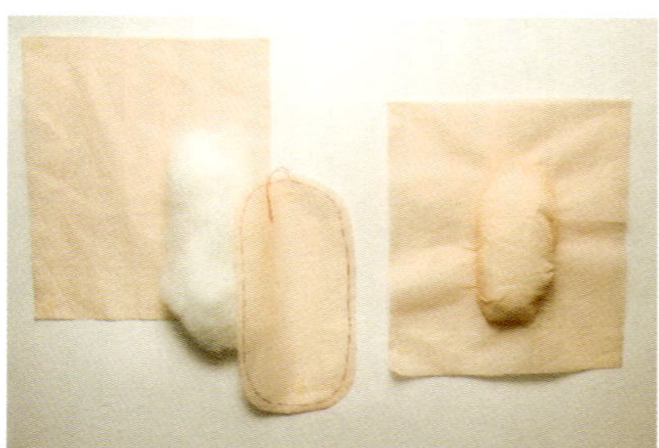

Bouillonne, shown in stages.

Painted Decoration

If you do not have the time or patience for embroidery, but still want to add a little detail to a plain silk or cotton, hand-painted decoration can be very effective and can be tailored to suit the cut of your dress. Painted decoration works well alone or combined with other techniques. If you plan to wash

your garment, make sure you use fabric paints or dyes and follow the instructions for fixing. Always test first to see how the ink reacts on the fabric. You may need to vary your design or change your brush if it bleeds out from the point on contact, which is more likely if you are using dyes. Paints tend to sit on the surface and give finer lines. I would suggest you trace your design in pencil or chalk before starting.

Quilting

Wadded quilting, as shown in Project 6, was commonly used in the eighteenth century for a range of items but primarily for warmth. Quilted petticoats became more fashionable later in the century and started to be shown and worn as outer garments. Wadded quilting was normally completed flat on a frame, using three layers: lining, wadding and fabric. Although I did not use a frame for the petticoat shown in Project 6, the process is much the same.

First, layer the fabrics flat, then pin and tack them, before tracing the pattern on with pencil, chalk or fabric pens, and finally use running stitch or backstitch to complete the design. The fabric is now ready to be made up.

The most common design was based on diamond shapes, from the simple style shown in this book to more complex designs in which each diamond is filled with further patterns. Again, I would suggest you look to originals for inspiration.

Quilting, showing the layers.

Ladies of fashion showing the changes towards the end of our timeline.

Fabrics

We went to every Mercer in Bath to match Mrs. Michel's Silk, but in vain. The Pattern is too old for Bath, but it may probably be matcht in London.

John Penrose[4]

The first step in creating a fashionable Georgian or Regency dress, then and now, is to choose your materials. The challenge for the modern maker is finding a fabric that could pass for period. Your choice of fabric can impact on how period your finished dress looks. A modern fabric will give your costume a completely different look to one appropriate for the period. Of course you can make up the patterns in this book in any fabric you wish. The following advice is aimed at those of you who are trying to achieve an authentic look.

There were a huge variety of fabrics available in the eighteenth century. Fabric was produced in a different way and hence the final product would look and feel very different. Although there are still some places producing fabric woven by hand, or on early machinery, this isn't what you are likely to find in your nearest fabric shop. The main difference between modern mass production fabric and period fabric is how it handles. The silk for the dress in Project 23 was woven on original early Victorian waterpowered machinery at a Georgian mill established in 1814 and the silk for the jacket was woven by hand.

It can be hard to try and match the fabric that you see original garments made from in museums or read about in contemporary accounts with what is on sale today. The names that fabrics were called then do not always relate to what we call them today. Looking at accounts of contemporary fabric can be quite confusing; there is quite a range of spellings used for the same thing. Many fabrics were sold under a trade name or named after their weave, and some after the place they were made. Although in the eighteenth century there was not the same range of fabrics as we have today, there were a lot of different mixes that are not as easy to find today.

Woven Fabrics

Most fabric is woven; weaving is a process in which two sets of yarns are interlaced at right angles to form a fabric or cloth. The longitudinal threads are called the warp and the lateral threads are the wefts. This process was completed by hand at the start of our timeline, but key innovations over this period meant cloth was woven by water or steam-powered machinery, overseen by workers, by the end of it. How the two threads are woven together dictates the pattern and texture of the cloth.

Cotton is a plant-based woven fabric. Contemporary types of cotton included calico, which could be spelt calicoe, chintzes, cambric, flannel and dimities. Originally imported from India, cotton started to be produced in Britain in the eighteenth century and by the end of our timeline it was an important export product on which many livelihoods depended. At the start of the century it was comparatively rare and expensive, but after James Hargreaves improved thread production by inventing the spinning jenny in the 1760s, cotton could be made to be much more robust and no longer needed to be mixed with other threads, such as linen and wool. Cotton dresses became very fashionable and also progressively more affordable towards the end of the century. Cotton was perfect for decoration with printed patterns as printing technology improved, moving from printing with wooden stamps to metal rollers. The resulting fabric become cheaper and printed cotton became fashionable and was accessible to most women. As cotton became cheaper and more women started to wear colourful prints, rich fashionable women turned to finer, less practical cottons such as fine Indian muslins, lawns and voiles.

Silk is a woven fabric made from thread from the cocoons of silkworms. Silk was used throughout our timeline, although it changed a great deal over this period. The fashionable silks become progressively lighter and the patterns become much smaller throughout the century. Italian

Samples of four printed and one woven cotton.

Samples of both printed and embroidered cottons and muslins.

brocades were fashionable at the start of the period, later to be overtaken by lighter, finer silks. Stripes became fashionable, as did pastel colours. By the end of our timeline silk weavers were copying cotton designs, as cotton rivalled silk in the fashion stakes when small sprig and spot patterns were the height of fashion. Silk was a status symbol and it was made into garments designed to be seen. The fact that it was not really washable or hard-wearing made it out of reach for many people. Silks were most commonly used for evening or court dresses, although they could also be used for smaller items such as reticules, parasols, fans, fichus and other fine accessories.

Samples of woven silk and cotton stripes.

Linen is a plant-based woven fabric, which was used throughout our period for a large range of stable garments. Linen was popular for underwear as it wicks sweat away from the body, making it very suitable for garments worn next to the skin; it is best to make your chemise from pure linen for this reason as it will keep you cool and dry on a hot day, whatever your overdress is made from. Linen was affordable, easy to wash and dye; it could be hard-wearing but also very fine. Fine, bright white, crisp linen trimmed with lace was a sign of wealth.

Skins and furs are animal hides. Leather was commonly made from the hides of cows, using a process called tanning. It was used for items such as gloves, shoes, corsets, hats and heavy-duty aprons. Thicker skins such as cowhide were used for items such as shoes, which needed to be hard-wearing, and finer skins such as calf were used for items such as gloves, which need to be flexible.

Wool is a fibre that comes from sheep. Wool production was one of the staple trades in Britain. It can be knitted, woven and felted and was used to make warm clothing for wearing at home and outer garments, as it is naturally warm and offered some protection from wet weather. Tailored suits such as riding habits were made from wool, and felted wool was used to make hats.

Finding the Right Fabric

Cottons are still woven and printed in India. Many of the traditional designs that would have been used in Georgian time are still printed today. South Asian fabric shops are a good place to look for good value printed cottons and linens and many are sold in lengths suitable for making up traditional costumes, such as the sari or salwar kameez. You will need to work this into your layplan calculations. Although silk is quite easy to find, it can be quite expensive. Hence South Asian fabric shops can also be a good place to look for reasonably priced silk. Plain silks are normally cheaper than patterned silks, so creating your own decorations can bring the price down. If you or someone you know travels a lot, make sure you check if they can buy fabric when they travel, as different places often specialize in different fabrics. Many towns and villages still have weekly markets or market days and I have been known to pick up a perfect length of fabric for an astounding price at market stalls. Many stallholders buy bankrupt stock in bulk and sell it on cheaply, meaning you can access fabrics you would not normally be able to dream of. The most wonderful thing about markets and independent shops is that you can engage in the historical art of haggling or negotiating for the price of items to be lowered. Although the mid Georgian period was also the time when the fixed price became established, an essential aspect of the high street experience was haggling. There are of course lots of great online fabric shops, although if you are unsure, it is often advisable to order a sample before making a purchase. Soft furnishing fabrics can provide solutions for the heavier fabric worn at the start of the century, but make sure to check to see if the fabric has been treated in any way as this can affect how it hangs.

If your eyes are larger then your purse, don't worry: many of my best fabric finds have been from charity shops or jumbles sales. Make sure everyone knows you are sewing period costumes and you will find you are handed down all sorted of treasures from people keen to clear out and find their old junk a new home.

Although big cities have more shops, it can be helpful to develop a rapport with your nearest store as this will be the place you go when you are stuck. If they know what you are looking for, they can keep an eye out for things they know you will like. I have found the best way to find the most suitable shop for something I need in a big city like London is to ask people who live there or have worked in the trade there for some time. Keep a note of any finds, as you will be surprised how easy they are to lose track of if you don't need to visit for a while.

Knowing other people with a similar interest can also be a great help, as you can swap fabrics as well as tips.

What to Look For

Be aware that many modern fabrics are mixed with synthetics, so for an authentic costume, make sure the fabric is pure. You should get a feel for different fabrics once you have been handling them for some time. If you are really unsure, ask for a sample and try the burn test. Look for flaws in the fabric while it is being measured and do not be afraid to point out anything you see. If you have to work around a flaw, the price should be dropped or extra fabric purchased to take this into account. Be aware of the width of your chosen fabric as this will affect how much fabric you need; this aspect is easy to overlook when shopping online. Period guides advise shoppers to choose their ball gown fabrics by candlelight, as they would rarely been seen in daylight. Although it may be unlikely, should you ever make a dress for a truly period evening event, this would be a good tip!

Practicalities

Cotton is a very practical fabric; it is easy to work with, washable, cheap and easy to find. As long as you prewash your fabric before making up your garment, you should be able to machine wash it. When working out what you need, allow about 3 per cent extra for shrinkage.

Some silks do mark if they get wet. These are not ideally suited for daily wear and must be carefully treated while making up. I do not advise beginners to use them. Other silks can be handwashed and some even go through the washing machine. If you are unsure how a fabric will wash, cut a small square and wash it. This will show you if it shrinks and how it washes.

Leather cannot be washed, but it does need to be fed. Just like polishing your shoes to make them last longer, leather feed helps to extend the life of gloves or a corset. Leather feed cannot be used on suede, which should only be brushed.

Sometimes trying to make something new from, say, a pair of old curtains or a retro nightie can feel like a lost cause, but remember: anyone can make a £500 length of silk look like an old rag. It takes real skill to make old rags look like Cinderella's dream dress, and practice is all you need to get there!

Trim
Trim
polonaise
standard
size
12
CF
Trim
The metric GRADER SQUARE
ACORLAN
Cms
Patterns
12

If it be made tight to the shape, every symmetrical line is discovered with a grace so decent, that vestals, without a blush, might adopt the chaste apparel.
Lady of Distinction, The Mirror of the Graces[1]

The Patterns

Taking care to make sure you locate and measure the right points on your body, compare your measurements to the standard pattern sizes, making a note of how much larger or smaller you are for each measurement.

Scale up the pattern to full size and cut out in the standard size. These patterns are all a size 12, which measures as follows:

Bust:	88cm
Waist:	72cm
Nape to waist:	20.6cm
Top arm:	28.4cm

Start by ensuring patterns and any extra paper you may be adding are pressed. If you are scaling the pattern up, I suggest you adjust your standard size pattern on top of another sheet of pattern paper. Once you have made all of the adjustments, you can use weights to keep the cut pieces in place while you trace your new pattern onto the paper below.

Divide the difference between your size and the standard size between the seams on your chosen pattern. This will tell you how much you need to add or take away from each point. If possible, try to avoid adding to or taking away from the centre front and centre back seams.

Following the examples shown here, cut and spread/shut each pattern piece until it matches the difference between your measurement and the standard pattern.

It is likely that your bust and waist measurement adjustments will not match those of the standard pattern, in which case spread or shut the pattern to the measurement required and draw in new curves as needed, following the line of the original pattern as shown. When an alteration interrupts a stitching line, make sure your new line is tapered gradually and smoothly into

Length: adding extra in.

Left: Toile, set square and pattern.

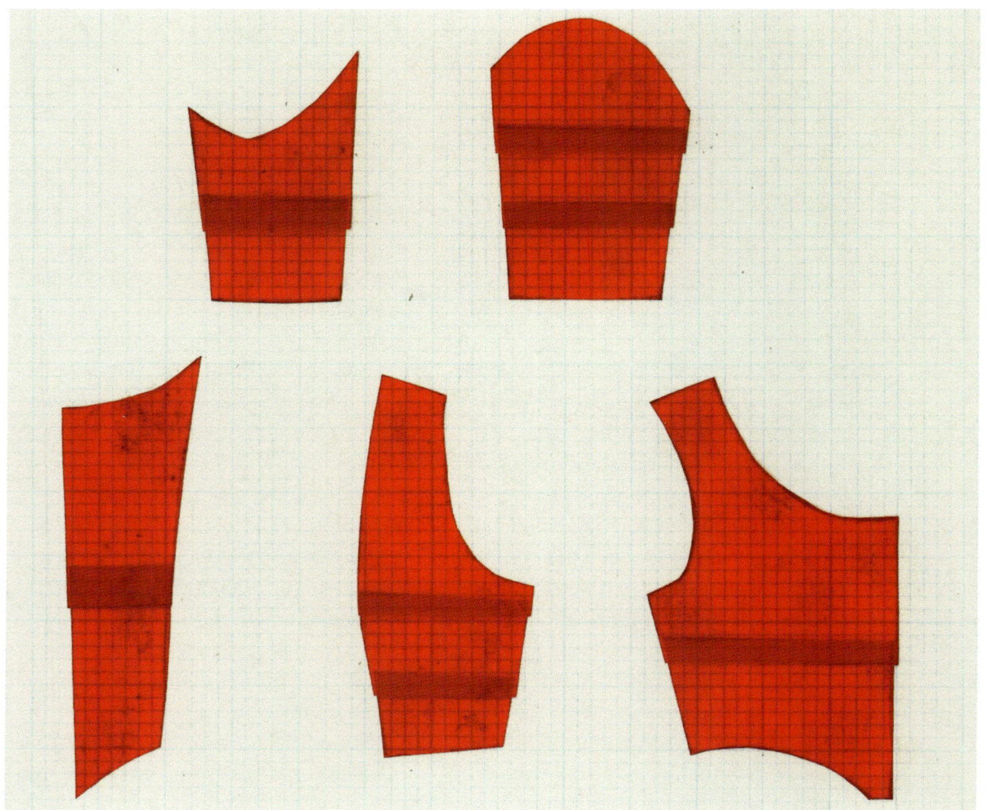

Length: taking away.

Width: adding extra in.

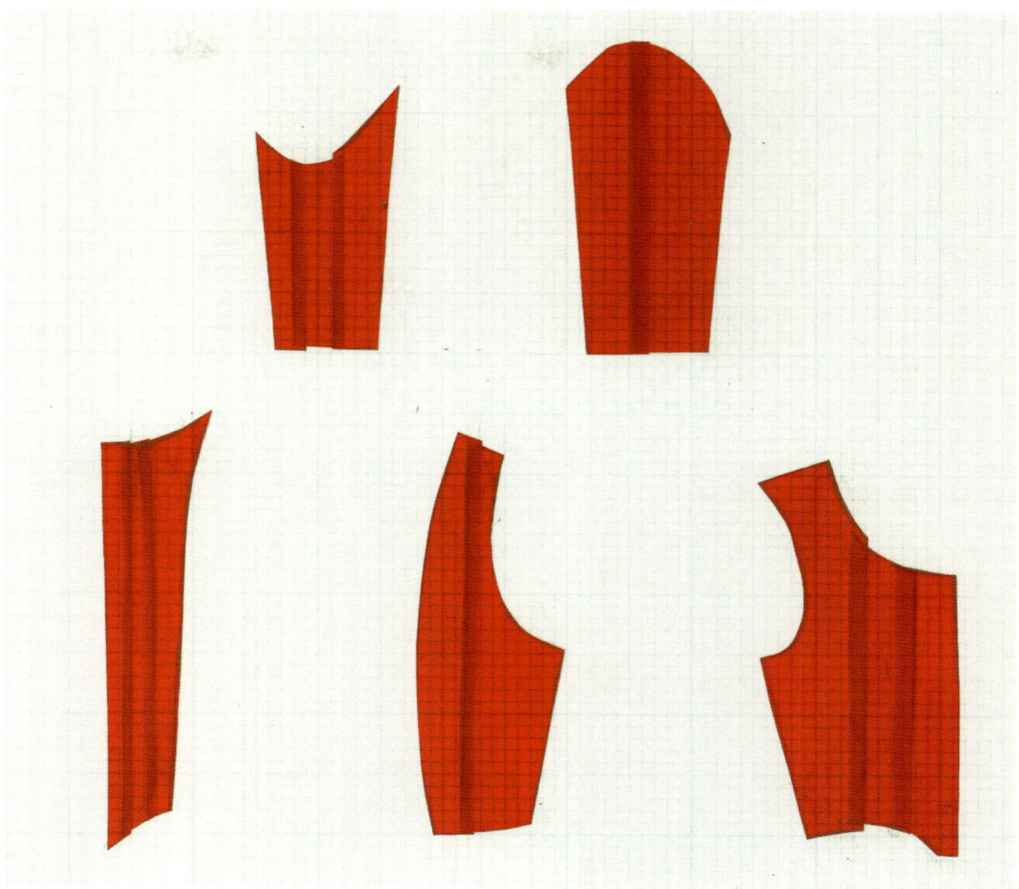

the original line. Also make sure you have transferred key markings such as the grain line to your new pattern.

When making more than one adjustment, change the length first and then the width to ensure the pattern lines up. If you change the armhole, then you must change the top of the sleeve to match, and vice versa. If you have to add or remove more than 2cm from the pattern, do so in more than one place on the pattern.

When you have finished making adjustments, draw off the new pattern or tape up the gaps. Your pattern is now ready for testing. Before you cut out a toile, you can match the edges of the paper pattern together to ensure the seams still match. A small difference does not mean your pattern will not fit; sometimes it is just a case of adding or taking away a little extra from a seam line.

The patterns in this book do not include any seam allowance. If you are used to using patterns which have seam allowances included, it is best to add them to your paper pattern, as it is all too easy to cut out your fabric before remembering to add them.

I always work with patterns without seam allowances, as it is easier to adjust them, and I can vary the seam allowances to suit the project. After I have pinned the pattern to the fabric, I draw the seam allowances directly onto the fabric with chalk.

Cutting Out

If you have made a toile and you are happy with the fit, you need not add more then 1.5cm to all the seams, apart from the hem, which should have more. How much more depends on what suits your fabric: 5cm is a good standard hem.

If you are prone to gaining weight, or expect the costume to be worn by different people, you can add a larger seam allowance of 2.5cm at the centre back and side seams. Costume designers routinely use these larger seam allowances as most costumes are reused again and again for different productions, and the larger seam allowance makes adjusting the costumes easier.

Before laying out your fabric to cut out, check for any marks or flaws that you want to avoid. Your fabric should be pressed before you cut it out, as should the pattern pieces. If the fabric is folded, ensure it is folded evenly, with the selvages meeting or the two cut ends meeting in the centre.

When cutting out, start by working out the length and width of the skirt panels required and then check you have enough space left to cut the bodice and sleeves from the remaining fabric. If not, you will need to adjust the fullness of your skirts, removing panels or adjusting the length, until you can fit everything in.

Your grain lines should match the straight grain of your fabric, unless they are to be cut on the bias. The easiest way of checking this is to measure from the top and bottom of the grain line to the fabric selvage edge. If the selvage is not straight you will need to look at the weave of the fabric to establish the straight grain. Folding your pattern piece in half can make this easer. Once you have the grain right, just pin the side touching the fabric and then fold the other side down and pin. It is worth taking your time to do this. If you are really short on fabric and do not have enough to keep the grain lines straight, take solace in the fact that there are many surviving garments that show the grain was not kept straight in the original garments. If you do choose to go down this route, I would suggest using a straight-cut backing fabric such as cotton to ensure this does not change the fit.

Before you pin your fabric, check your pins will not leave a visible hole in the fabric. If so, you will need to use chalk and weights to mark pattern pieces instead. Use weights to smooth out larger pattern pieces and pin around the edges of the pattern,

Once you have altered and scaled up your pattern, it may help you to add notches to your pattern pieces. Notches are little arrowheads on the edges of your pattern to show you where to snip the fabric to help you establish which piece is stitched to which once you have removed the pattern from the fabric. If you get muddled, refer back to the original patterns in the book, which are laid out in order with seams that are stitched together next to each other. This can also help if you forget which way up a piece should go.

making sure the centre doesn't bubble up and there are no creases or tucks in the fabric. Double-check everything before cutting your fabric and keep the fabric flat whilst cutting.

Working with Prints

If your fabric is patterned, you also need to decide if you want to match up the print at the seams. There are period examples of both matched and

unmatched prints, so the final decision can be down to whether you have enough fabric and how it will look on the finished garment. If you are struggling to visualize this, try pinning the fabric to your mannequin to give you a better idea of the finished effect. Make sure you transfer any markings needed to your fabric before removing the pattern pieces. I like to leave the pattern pieces on the fabric right up until I am ready to pin, tack and stitch them. This ensures I don't muddle the face side and the wrong side, or how much seam allowance I have marked.

Keeping Order

Keep all your pattern pieces together when you're not using them to ensure nothing goes missing. Hang on to your scraps of fabric, or 'cabbage' as it was called, as this is useful for testing stitches and for making textile decorations. It was common practice in the eighteenth century that when you took a length of fabric to a maker to have it made into a garment, you then also received a bundle of the leftover cabbage with the finished garment. It was said that this was because past customers had seen the maker wearing a waistcoat skillfully patched together from their fabric!

The author and stylist adjust Camille's sleeve during the shoot.

Getting the Right Fit

The result of the finest toilet should be an elegant women, not an elegantly dressed woman.

Lady of Distinction, The Mirror of the Graces[2]

No matter how beautiful the fabric, or how neat your stitching, your finished costume will not look its best unless it fits you well. In addition to fitting your body, your dress should also be cut to suit your proportions. When making a pattern for the first time, it is a good idea to make a test garment or toile as it is called in the industry. A toile is made from a cheap piece of fabric, which is similar in weight to your final material; calico is commonly used. Before you cut out your toile, look at your final fabric. Is it patterned? In which direction do you want the pattern to go? If it is striped, do you want the centre back or front panels cut on the bias, so that the stripes meet in a v pattern in the centre? If so, you need cut the toile in the same way. Fabric cut on the bias reacts differently to that cut on the straight grain as it has more give, which can affect the fit of the garment.

The Bodice

The fit around the bodice and sleeves is the closest and as such the best place to start. The one exception to this is Project 2: the *robe volante*, but do not make the mistake of thinking that as this is loose-fitting it will not need testing. Loose-fitting garments still need to fit well. If you do not want to make a full toile for your *volante*, I suggest cutting the pattern off at hip level and establishing the fit around the torso and sleeves in the same way as I describe for the fitted bodices. This can also be done for any dresses that do not have a waist seam but for which you only wish to make a toile for the bodice.

Once you have adjusted the standard pattern to your size, the next stage is to cut and stitch together a bodice and sleeve. If your shoulders and arms are symmetrical you need only cut one sleeve, but if you are aware that there is a difference between them, which is quite common, it's best to cut two. You can stitch your toile together by hand

Stripes cut on the bias at the back of a Spencer jacket.

or machine, but it is best to use a larger, looser stitch to make it easier for you to unpick if needed. You don't need to stitch the sleeve into the bodice; it is best to check the fit and adjust the sleeve into the bodice while you are wearing it. Ideally you would have another person to help check the fit while you observe in a mirror, but if you have a mannequin in your size, you can check the fit on this. You can also stitch your cuff to your sleeve at this stage, or if you are unsure and want to play with the scale of the frills on your cuff, you can keep it separate and pin it on after you have fitted the sleeve. It is also important that you put on the undergarments you intend to wear under the finished costume, or that you dress the mannequin in these. Make sure you spend a bit of time laced into your corset, so you are sure that you are happy with the fit, before you move onto your outer garments.

Start by putting the bodice on and pinning it closed at the openings. If you plan to have a bodice with a stomacher and laced or tied front, you can pin the stomacher in for a closer estimation of how the finished garment will look. You can also add ties or laces to your toile. Use a leather punch to add the needed holes to your toile and then rub a candle over each side of the holes. The wax will stop them fraying or ripping during the fitting. You are looking for as close a fit as is comfortable, so pin in the seams if the garment is too large. Spread the extra fabric across more than one seam if the adjustment is large, say over 2.5cm. If the bodice is too small, measure the gap and mark it onto the toile in pencil, adding the extra required across each seam on future patterns. Make sure you make a note of all adjustments ether directly onto the toile or in a notebook, as pins can fall out!

The Sleeves

Once you are happy with the fit of the bodice, slip on the sleeve and pin it in, matching the notches and being careful not to prick your skin. Your sleeve head should be larger than the bodice armhole it is to be fitted into. This extra fabric is firstly for ease, which enables you to move your arms, and secondly for fullness, which is part of the style of the sleeve. Puffed sleeves have a lot more fullness than fitted sleeves. Spread any additional fullness in the sleeve between the areas marked on the pattern, evening it out between the pins. The sleeve should have a closer fit than a modern sleeve, so do not expect to be able to wave your arms above your head. The close fit under the armpit, combined with corsetry makes this near impossible and out of character for the period. You should have enough give to move your arms up from your sides to the height of your bust and forward as if to take something from someone, so now is the time to test out any period dance steps you plan to do. Adjust the sleeve until it is comfortable and then mark the stitching line onto both the sleeve and the bodice with a pencil.

Sleeves of this period were often made up separately to the body and pinned in. This allowed different sleeves to be worn for different occasions, or for replacements to be made once the originals become worn or torn. This isn't the most practical arrangement for modern-day wear, as it not only adds extra time to dressing, it also increases the chance that the sharp end of a pin might find its way into your skin. Pins can also damage the fabric, as Mrs Allen discovered in Jane Austen's *Northanger Abbey*.

My dear Catherine, said she, do take this pin out of my sleeve: I am afraid it has torn a hole already.[2]

I would suggest you stitch your sleeves into the bodice.

When fitting a modern-day sleeve it is standard practice to use a running stitch to make gathers and to help ease the sleeve into the armhole. If you try this with a historical costume you will end up with a modern-looking sleeve. Instead, ease the extra fabric into the armhole between the pins, and stitch it in by hand for a period look. If you are unsure of the style or scale of your

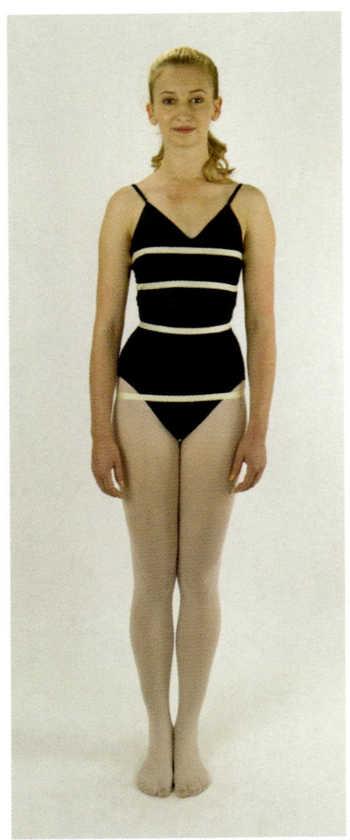

Showing the placement of the bust, underbust, waist and hip lines.

cuffs, now is a good time to experiment. You can pin on different styles or add trims of different sizes to establish which would best suit. Once you are happy with the sleeve fit, remove it, stitch the sleeve in, and try the toile on again to double-check the fit.

Before you remove your toile, have a good look at where the garment sits in comparison to key points on your body, that is your bust, waist and hip. Is the neckline in the most flattering position for your bust or would it be best a little higher or lower? How does the garment's waistline sit in comparison to your own? As the waistline on modern garments varies so much, it can be helpful to use string or cotton tape to find your natural waist. When fitting a higher Directoire-style bodice you can use cotton tape to mark where the waistline should sit on top of your corset before fitting the bodice. This gives you a line to refer to while fitting the bodice, especially when working with lighter fabrics such as muslin.

The Skirt

If you have some experience of making these, you may choose to save time and fabric by not making up a toile of the skirt. If you are at all unsure, I would suggest you make a full toile as you can always unpick and reuse the skirt fabric for future toiles. If you do not make a toile, be sure to double-check how full you want the skirt and how long it needs to be, making sure you allow at least 7.5cm for the hem. Remember: you can always take it up, but you can't stitch it back on! The fullness and the length are the two main things to look

The author adjusts Alison's skirt during the shoot.

for in a skirt toile.

If you are making a formal *robe de cour*, as in Project 5, the shape of the skirt is very much dictated by the panniers. It can help to drape your final fabric over the panniers while you are wearing them. This will give you an idea of what looks best with regard to issues such as front openings, textile decoration and hem lengths.

Pleats

When making eighteenth-century dresses, lots of people get confused by the classic Watteau pleats of the sack back gown. These are shown in this book in Project 4: the *robe à la française* and Project 2: the *robe volante*. The scale of these pleats often needs to be adjusted to suit the wearer and/or the scale of any patterns on the fabric. Should you find yourself in this situation, a toile on which all of the pattern marking have been transferred can be invaluable in helping to establish what needs changing, such as how much fabric needs to be added or taken away from the centre back seam and where the new points of reference are on your adjusted pattern.

Finding what Suits

When purchasing modern clothes most people have some idea of how their proportions vary from the standard for their size. Whether you are longer in your body or your legs, taller or shorter than the standard for your dress size, top or bottom heavy or straight up and down, the best thing about making any item of clothing is that you can adjust it to disguise or accentuate whatever you choose. The main trap people fall into when trying to disguise any aspects of themselves they are unhappy with is that they think too much about what they see as the problem and then struggle to see past it. For example, if you are petite but wish to look taller, you may assume you should wear small prints and avoid larger ones as you fear large prints will make you look even smaller. But actually, the opposite is often true, with small prints making a

The author adjusts Alison's pleats during the shoot.

Showing the structure of a Watteau pleat, with box pleats shown open and closed.

petite person look even more petite, and larger prints making more of an impact. Modern-style advice likes to give people lots of rules to follow: never wear this if you look like this, but always wear this, and so on. People feel safe following rules, but a lot of the time these simply are not true. By playing with placement and making small adjustments, a trained eye can make all styles suit all shapes and sizes. The key is to be aware of what suits you, work around the bits you like and be confident in your choices. If you are unsure, ask a friend. It is often easier to see what best suits someone else rather than what suits us. If you are struggling to make a decision, try taking pictures and looking at the effect on screen as this often helps to give a different perspective.

Returning to our toile, you will find by making small changes you can adjust the proportions of your dress to best suit yourself. For example, if you are tall and small-busted, moving the waist of your Directoire dress down 2.5cm or so will look much more flattering. If you don't have the fashionable Georgian curves, don't be afraid to using padding. Make small bust pads from wadding and place them under the bust before lacing up your corset. If you have broad shoulders, try lifting full sleeves higher onto your shoulder seam by moving the sleeve head 2.5cm closer to your neck. Making your toile is the stage when you should experiment with what best suits you, not when you are making your final garment. Make sure you note down any decisions you make as this will save you time in future.

Once you have removed the toile, you can transfer the markings onto your pattern. It is best to do this straight away, while it is fresh in your mind, but if you expect to be interrupted, make sure you make a note of the needed changes as you go along. If your weight fluctuates, you should consider allowing an extra seam allowance on the centre back and side seams to allow you to let your dress out at a later date. If you find you

Stays with bust pads.

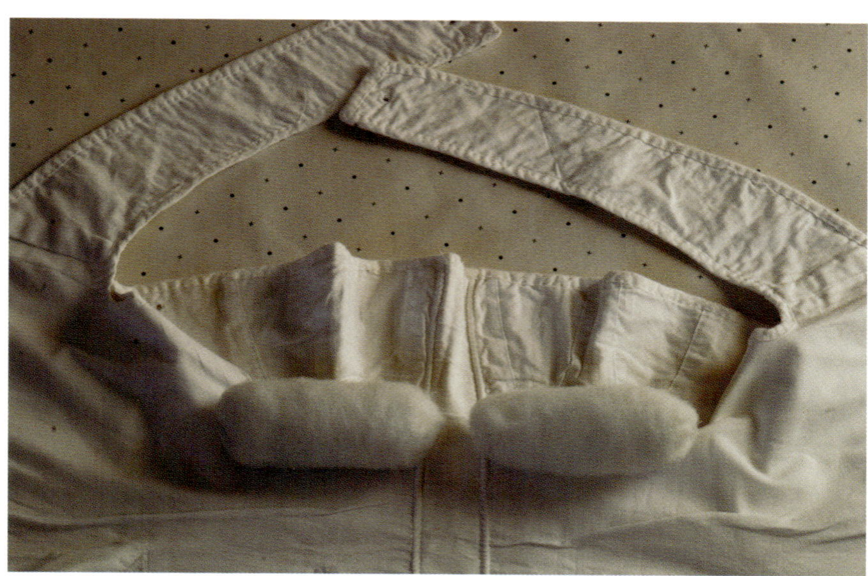

Showing placement of bust pads inside stays.

need to make quite a few changes, or they are quite large, it is best to make a second toile before you cut into your final fabric. You will then save time in the long run by developing a well-fitting pattern that you can use again and again.

Keeping a Record

Once you have a finished a pattern, it is worth taking time to write on each piece what it is, whom it is for and the date it was made. Keep all of the pieces together in a sleeve or envelope with the toile. If you intend to use the pattern a lot, it might be worth tracing it off onto card to help it stand up to repeated handling.

It can be very frustrating, when you start out to have to spend days on your toile when you are keen to get started on your final fabric, especially when you see professionals draw straight onto fabric and cut out a finished garment without a second thought. However, it is well worth taking your time over the toile, checking and double-checking each seam to ensure you don't have any problems when you come to fitting the final garment. The more things you make, the quicker and more confident you will become!

Chapter 5 – Underpinnings and Accessories 

Underpinnings

Every shape needs a solid foundation to support and strengthen it. Underwear at this time creates the external shape as well as protecting delicate fabrics from the body and the body from the often-harsh textures of fabrics woven with metallic threads, covered in glass beads and iron sequins. However you look at it, each item of underwear in a lady's wardrobe had a fundamentally practical role.

With all of these layers, getting dressed was a much greater undertaking than it is today. Many women needed help to get dressed and items had to be put on in the right order and worn in the right way to achieve the right effect. With all the layers in place, the gown never touched the skin. Each project lists the ideal underwear items to be worn with each outfit, although a corset and chemise is a good place to start. Patterns for underpinnings can be found in Chapter 16.

I will be discussing each item in the order that they would have been worn, starting with the first garment: the chemise, shift or smock.

Shift

And, first, a dirty smock appear'd,
Beneath the arm-pits well besmear'd;
Strephon, the rogue, display'd it wide,
And turn'd it round on ev'ry side:
On such a point, few words are best,
And Strephon bids us guess the rest;
But swears, how damnably the men lie
In calling Celia sweet and cleanly

'The Ladies Dressing Room',
Jonathan Swift[2]

A simple shift: the base garment.

The shift, later called the chemise, is the base garment, worn next to the skin and made from linen. It was the most frequently washed garment, and most women, unlike Swift's Celia, took pride in having a clean, white, starched shift as the neckline and cuffs were also often on show. The finest chemises were made from Holland linen and were trimmed with lace. The shape of the chemises didn't change a great deal over our timeline. At the start of the timeline chemises were plain with full sleeves and a frill at the neck. They were knee-length with a wide neckline, which just covered the shoulders. Sometimes the neckline would have a drawstring or pleats to pull in the

fullness and help keep it on. The full, gathered sleeves remained until about the 1740s when outer sleeves became fitted. With the slimmer fashions at the turn of the century, the chemise became straighter with a square neckline and short sleeves.

Original chemises needed to cope with the body's sweat. The armpits were most likely to mark the garment, so squares of fabric called gussets were cut and stitched into the chemise separately so that they could be easily replaced to prolong the life of the garment. Modern costume wearers don't have the same challenges, with deodorants and washing machines now available, so you can choose to cut your chemise with or without gussets: with is more authentic; without is simpler.

County fairs would have competitions for local women to win a smock, often a fine one that would have been outside their normal reach. Women often had to race to win and competition was fierce.

Stockings

Elizabeth continued her walk alone, crossing field after field at a quick pace, jumping over stiles and springing over puddles with impatient activity, and finding herself at last within view of the house, with weary ankles, dirty stockings, and a face glowing with the warmth of exercise.

Pride and Prejudice, Jane Austen[3]

Stockings were knitted on a frame. They were generally knitted by men and seamed together by women, and could be made from wool, cotton or silk. Developments in knitting machines meant that by the 1750s more complex designs could be incorporated into stockings. Gowns with skirts slightly shorter at the front could show off the bright colours and patterns of the stockings and shoes. Although stockings were often ribbed, they could not stay up on their own, so ribbons were tied around the top to keep them in place. The easiest place to tie your ribbon is just above the knee. Once you have tied the ribbon, turn the stocking down over the ribbon. Today we have Lycra and, if you prefer, you can buy stockings with stretch in, or wear tights.

Drawers

Drawers or bloomers started to be worn from the beginning of the 1800s. These open drawers had two separate legs joined by a waistband. Initially they were unpopular. One regency lady stated: 'They are the ugliest thing I ever saw; I will never put them on again.' They also presented new challenges as she goes on to say:

> I lost one leg in the street and did not deem it proper to pick it up again. Walked off leaving it in the street.
>
> *C. Willett Cunnington,*
> *The Perfect Lady* [4]

But they gained popularity in the Victorian era, when they were patronized by the Queen herself. They were fairly standard by 1830.

Stays

Stays or corsets held the torso in and created the shape of the bodice. Stays were often heavily boned, but were not tightly laced, as the metal eyelet had not yet been invented. However, as they were rigid and worn from childhood, this compressed the ribcage as girls grew, changing the shape of their bodies permanently. Stays were normally made by professional stay makers, although they were also sold ready made and exported from Britain to other countries. They normally consisted of two inner layers of linen plus an extra layer for the lining as well as the face fabric. Corsets were made from leather and brocade as well as linens and silks. Lightly boned stays were called jumps.

At the start of our time period, stays were long with tabs over the waist and remained so until the 1790s, when rising waistlines enabled shorter stays to be worn. Stays were essential for formal dress and they are the item of underwear that will make the most difference to how historically accurate your costume looks. All corsets change the shape of the body, but a well-fitted corset – much like a bra – should be comfortable to wear. Many women enjoy the additional support it gives. There were quite a lot of changes over the time period of this book, but the two patterns given can be adapted to be worn under all of the dresses.

Petticoat

> And her petticoat; I hope you saw her petticoat, six inches deep in mud, I am absolutely certain; and the gown which had been let down to hide it, not doing its office.
>
> *Pride and Prejudice, Jane Austen* [5]

I doubt its purpose interested Lizzy Bennet, but the reason for the petticoat was to protect the gown from the body and any dirty surfaces you walked over, as well as to help create the overall shape of the gown and to keep you warm. Petticoats were commonly made from linen and later cotton. Red flannel petticoats were popular as they were seen to be particularly warm. Petticoats started to be piped with cord to make them stiffer and wider from the 1820s. A petticoat would be worn under and over large hoops.

Longline leather stays, shown from the back.

Longline leather stays, shown from the front.

Short stays, shown from the front.

Short stays, shown from the back.

A simple petticoat.

A late Regency/early Victorian corded petticoat.

At this time, the difference between a petticoat and skirt was small, with the open gown dominating the first half of the eighteenth century. The difference is that a skirt goes over the top of the petticoat, which could be designed not to be seen or it could be fancy and designed to be shown off. Either version is called a petticoat. Both skirts and petticoats were generally cut in the same manner, being straight without gores. These are basically squares or rectangles and you adapt the shapes to change the fullness of your petticoat. The three patterns in the book cover a standard width petticoat, a wide petticoat to be worn over the top of a hoop, and a slim petticoat for later styles.

Hoops

The first panniers or hoops were bell-shaped, not dissimilar to the crinolines of the Victorian era. These became fashionable after the fashion for skirts with tails became popular. It was not long before they started to evolve and by 1720 they were oval-shaped. By 1730 the front had become flattened and tied with cords and in the 1740s hoops were at their widest. Afterwards they again became smaller. All classes of women wore hoops; servants simply wore smaller versions than their mistresses. The boning in hoops was whalebone or wood. For the hoops in this book I have used metal and the fabric is linen or stiffened canvas, although I have also used drill cotton and canvas.

The large hoops shown in this book are in the English style, shaped like a kidney bean when looked at from above. French hoops were flat across the front. The shapes varied a little from country to country, but the shape can be adjusted by varying the tightness of the boning and the tapes inside the hoops.

Side or pocket hoops were developed to flatten when you sit down, enabling women to sit easily and take up less space when sitting. They also take up less space when not worn.

Hoops are worn over the top of the

Large hoops, shown from the front.

Large hoops, shown from the side.

Large hoops, shown
from the back.

corset; they are tied around the waist or looped onto the stays. When dressing, it is easy to tie them too high, right on the waist, when they should be tied to sit on the hip. If they are too high, they shorten the body, and the waist shape is lost altogether.

Pocket hoops, shown from the front.

Pocket hoops, shown from the side.

Pocket hoops, shown from the back.

Pads

Up goes her hand, and off she slips
The bolsters that supply her hips.

*'A Beautiful Young Nymph Going to
Bed', Jonathan Swift*[6]

From about 1770 onwards, hoops were replaced by pads, which like hoops are worn over the top of the corset. Small pads were first worn at the rear of a large hoop to support the back and stop it slipping. Like hoops, pads should not be worn too high on the waist, or the waist is lost all together. They must be tied around the waist to hang at hip level.

Twin pads, shown from the front.

Twin pads, shown from the side.

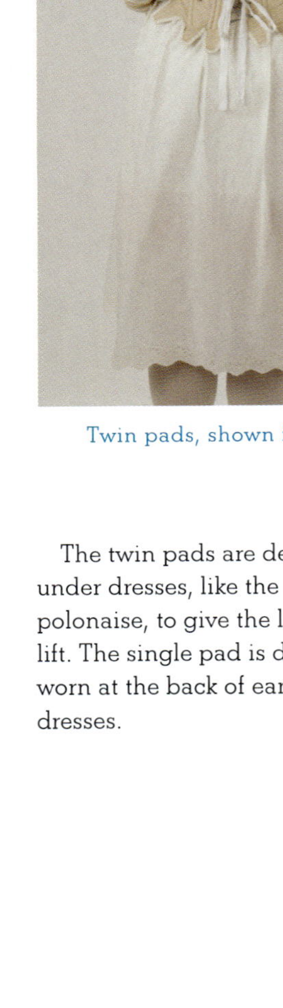

Twin pads, shown from the back.

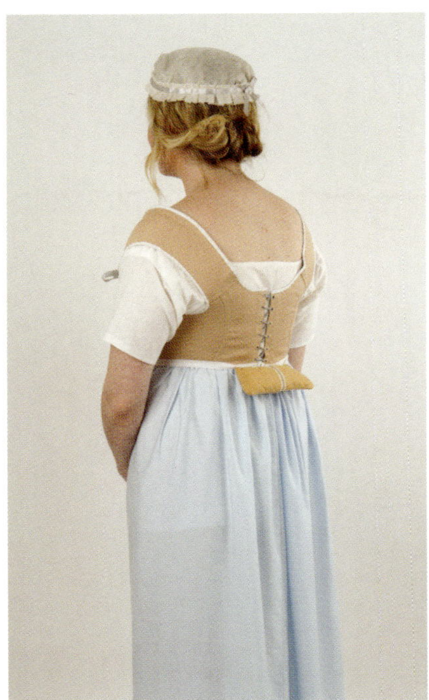

A single pad, shown from the side.

A single pad, shown from the back.

The twin pads are designed to go under dresses, like the robe à la polonaise, to give the looped-up skirts a lift. The single pad is designed to be worn at the back of early Regency dresses.

Bryony decides which shoes to wear.

Chapter 16. It is impossible to cover every item, or provide patterns and instructions for everything mentioned, but I have tried to write a little about each of the key items that you might want to use to complete your costumes. Items are divided by where on the body they are worn or held.

Torso

POCKETS

Pockets sit somewhere between underwear and accessories. They are half modern pockets and half bag, and are worn tied around the waist, over the chemise but under the skirts. Slits in the skirts would allow the wearer to reach their pockets. Worn singularly or in pairs, they could be quite large and still be fully disguised by the bulk of the skirts, whilst still allowing a woman to carry everything she needed for the day. Although they were not seen, surviving examples are often richly embroidered. At the end of the century when the skirts slimmed down, pockets were no longer practical and the

An embroidered pocket worn by Kirsten and made by Rachel Parton.

Accessories

I assure you ... she has all Paris in her disposal; the sweetest caps! The most beautiful trimmings! And her ribbons are quite divine! It is the most dangerous thing you can conceive to go near her; I never trust myself in her room but I am sure to be ruined. If you please, I'll take you to her this morning.

Cecillia, Fanny Burney[7]

In the eighteenth century accessories did more than just complete an outfit; they had a language all of their own. They were an important measure of etiquette and breeding and aided friendship and courtship.

The task of fully fashioning yourself as an eighteenth-century woman is a daunting one. Originally it would have involved trips to a great many different specialists. Buying just the items mentioned in this chapter would involve visits to the haberdasher, milliner, glover, shoemaker, jeweller, hairdresser and wig-maker. So when starting out, you should not expect to be able to make everything yourself. Many of these items would have been made at home and could make sewing suitable projects. Others you may be able to beg, borrow or pick up cheaply, whilst some you may simply choose to hire.

Accessory patterns can be found in

reticule became the beginning of the modern handbag. The pocket never returned to favour, but it's remembered in the nursery rhyme about a little girl whose pocket ribbon becomes untied. It is also still used as a reference for a child who frequently loses things:

> Lucy Locket lost her pocket,
> Kitty Fisher found it;
> Not a penny was there in it,
> Only ribbon round it.

APRONS

> I don't feel at home in my own house without an apron.
>
> *Lady Hartford*[8]

The model wears a fine lace-trimmed apron.

At this time, aprons were more than just an item to keep you clean while working. In the eighteenth century aprons become a fashion accessory in their own right, and impractical but beautiful elaborate aprons were worn. Aprons also held another symbolism at a time when maternity clothes did not exist. Laces were loosened and any gaps were covered with an apron tied over the bump. When a women was seen suddenly wearing an apron, rumors of pregnancy soon followed.

CAPES

As gowns were so full, capes were the most practical items for providing warmth outdoors. Fitted coats and jackets became fashionable with the slim dresses at the turn of the century. Hoods on capes also had to change during the eighteenth century to accommodate ever-growing hairstyles. They were also worn for masquerades to disguise the wearer and their costume.

SHAWLS

> She had from three to four hundred shawls ... she always wore one in the morning which she draped over her shoulder more gracefully than anyone else I have ever known.
>
> *Mme De Remuset on Joséphine de Beauharnais*[9]

Shawls become more practical and fashionable with the slimmer, lighter gowns at the end of the century. They provided warmth and colour to a period dominated by white dresses. Modern shawls that look suitably period, as the fabrics and patterns used have not changed a great deal, can still be found. Period paintings can give lots of different ideas on how to drape your shawl.

NECKERCHIEF

> Their neckerchiefs were puffed up so high that their noses were scarcely visible.
>
> *Sophie De La Roche*[10]

The neckerchief is also called a fichu, which is French for handkerchief or a kerchief. It is basically a triangle worn around the neck and shoulders. Neckerchiefs often had long ends, which could be caught up by the stomacher ties in the front of the bodice and held securely. It was similar to a tucker, which is a triangle tucked into the front of the bodice for modesty, It was fashionable to match the sleeve lace with that on the cap and tucker.

Hands

RETICULE

Once skirts become so slim that a pocket could no longer be hidden, the modern handbag was born in the form of the reticule. This started life as a simple drawstring bag very much like the pocket and became ever more

Bryony carries a reticule, the first handbag.

decorative and complex as it evolved. These are simple to make and a great starting place for beginners.

GLOVES AND MITTS

Gloves were generally elbow-length, quite plain and commonly made from soft leather, cotton or silk. They were worn for all formal occasions. Mitts are fingerless gloves that women wore indoors and kept hands warm while leaving the fingers free to complete activities such as playing cards or writing letters. Glove-making is a complex skill, but some modern gloves can look period, and you may even find vintage leather gloves that would suit. Try to avoid gloves that are very shiny or too loosely fitted.

FANS

My body is but composed of long
bones
And I had all the time but skin on the
bones
I shine in company, and without any
rest,
In the height of the summer, I am at
all the parties.

Riddle about the fan, origin unknown

Fans had a practical use in keeping you cool in a warm ballroom, but they also developed a wide range of other uses. Printed fans would also be used for commemorating a national victory, to declare a political alliance or even for offering a useful reminder of the latest dance steps.

More meaning was given to the fan when a language was developed from the different motions of the fan. This was to become ever more complex in the nineteenth century, when women would also pass time by interpreting the shapes and motifs on their fans to predict each others futures.

You can still buy fans today and period examples turn up in the strangest places, so it is always a good idea to keep an eye out on your travels. You can now also buy kits to paint or cover your own fan to match with the rest of your outfit.

PARASOLS

Elizabeth obeyed, and running into her own room for her parasol, attended her noble guest downstairs.

Pride and Prejudice, Jane Austen[11]

In a time when having a tan marked you out as a manual worker, keeping the sun off your face and preserving your delicate complexion was key. A parasol served this purpose, while also offering the opportunity to perfect your walking costume. They often feature in fashion plates of the time with costumes designed for outdoor use such as the *robe à la polonaise*. You can buy replica or vintage parasols, or if you are feeling adventurous, buy a kit and cover your own.

MUFFS

This was an accessory designed to help keep your hands warm. Muffs were small until the 1770s, when they became larger and started to have pockets inside for other items. Muffs could be made from silk, feathers, velvet or fur.

Georgia and Alison ready for a masked ball.

Alison carries a parasol to keep off the sun.

The model keeps her hands warm with a decorative muff.

Pump shoes were often tied on with a ribbon, like modern ballet shoes.

Feet

SHOES

Shoes in 1710 had heels and pointed toes. They were generally closed by 1740 and more dedicate with a lower heel. They were often ornate, made up in fabric to match a dress with elegant heels. Most shoes were done up with buckles by this stage. Buckles could be very decorative and were highly valued items that could also be used on different pairs of shoes. Heels were at their highest between the 1770s and 1780s. Shoes became lower and simpler in the late 1780s to match the changing fashions, and by the close of the century they were flat with thin soles, much like today's ballet pumps, Tied with ribbons, they were not practical for outdoor activities, when leather boots would be worn instead. It can be quite hard to find cheap alternatives to the early styles, which are quite different from the many styles on sale today. The closest match you may be able to find is a court shoe with added bows or buckles. Later styles are much easier to cheat, but it is always worth looking in the sales as you never know what you may find. If you plan to spend a lot of time standing or dancing in your shoes, it may be worth saving up and investing in a replica pair. For the photos in this book, where the shoes were needed for just one day, we hired them, which is another option for short-term use.

For information on stockings see Chapter 5.

Head

HATS

> At the milliners, the ladies we met were so much dressed, that I should rather have imagined they were making visits than purchases.
>
> *Evelina, Frances Burney*[12]

The milliner, perhaps more than any other maker, had to have their finger on the ever-changing pulse of fashion and respond with continued changes to their creations. After all, hats were cheaper than a new outfit and much

Bryony is holding a poke bonnet, which would be tied on with a ribbon.

Kirsten is holding a straw hat trimmed with a ribbon.

easier to re-dress, as Lydia highlights in *Pride and Prejudice*:

> 'Look here, I have bought this bonnet. I do not think it is very pretty; but I thought I might as well buy it as not. I shall pull it to pieces as soon as I get home, and see if I can make it up any better.'

Lace, ruffles, tippets, feathers, flowers and ribbons could all be added, removed or readjusted according to the whims of the current fashion. This is also something you can do once you have a basic shape to work with.

Hats were always worn outdoors, and by the 1780s hats were worn with all but full dress. As fashions become slimmer at the end of the century, hats become more elaborate. Hats that fitted closely around the face, fashionable in the Regency and early Victorian periods, were called bonnets and these became quite large, as Jane Austen

herself noted:

> I am amused by the present style of female dress; the coloured petticoats with braces over the white Spencer's and enormous bonnets upon the full stretch are quite entertaining.

> *Pride and Prejudice*, Jane Austen[13]

Caps or coifs were worn to cover the head when inside the house. These were also often worn under outdoors hats as well. Larger styles were worn at night. Styles varied a great deal from the very large to very simple small ones; however, larger hairstyles did present a challenge:

> More Miss Mirvan cannot wear one of the caps she made, because they dress her hair too large for them.

> *Evelina*, Frances Burney[14]

Kirsten wears an indoor coif cap or nightcap.

HEADRESSES

A fontange was a high headdress popular in the late seventeenth- and early eighteenth-century Europe. Often supported by a wire frame, the headdress was a collection of pleats, ribbons and bows. It was frequently called a topknot in England and a version of this fashion was worn by women from all levels of society. It is said to have been named after Louis XIV's mistress, the Marquise de Fontange.

TURBANS

Turbans become fashionable in the eighteenth century, as visitors to Turkey and the Orient returned with details of

With the centre of the shawl over your head twist the edges all the way down to the ends.

Next, one by one wrap them round the top of you head and down the back.

Overlap the ends and tie behind your head to secure.

Tuck any extra bits into the back of your turban.

Your turban is down complete.

Turban shown from the side.

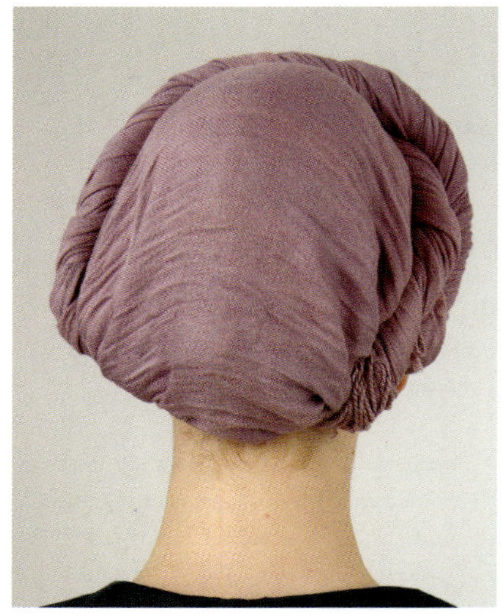
The back of the finished turban.

Decorate with feathers and brooches or whatever you wish.

this exotic clothing. Turkish dress became very fashionable for masquerade costumes in the eighteenth century. The turban was an item that moved across into normal wear and soon many fashion leaders were painted wearing their versions of the turban. By the end of the century the turban was an established fashion item. There are limitless ways to tie and decorate a turban for period wear; the example shown is a nearly foolproof way of tying a turban. I have lost count of the times I have had to remove and re-tie my turban, or tie them on others at events, and it returns to the right shape every time – even without a mirror.

HAIR AND WIGS

> I have just had my hair dressed. You can't imagine how oddly my head feels; full of powder and black pins, and a great cushion on top of it.
>
> *Evelina, Frances Burney*[15]

At the start of our time period, height was created with fontange headdresses, whilst hair was dressed in tight hanging curls with a centre parting. Hair soon started to be worn up in ever tighter curls, close to the head, with the bulk of the hair being worn round the

Kirsten's own hair styled in a high late Georgian fashion.

back. By the 1760s highly powdered natural hair moves to the top of the head from the back, and by 1765 pads are being used. In the late 1760s wigs are common. Wigs are at their most absurd between the 1770s and 1780s. Hair is still large in the 1790s but it becomes looser and simpler, and by the turn of the century real hair, which was often shaved to aid wig-wearing, is fashionable again. Short curls remain and are worn brushed forward onto the face, but soon become longer curls, with the bulk of the hair being worn at the back of the head again. The 1820s and 1830s mark another experimental period in hairdressing when the centre parting is once again fashionable with all sorts of fanciful creations worn on top of the head.

The styles in this book are all created using the models' own hair, which was often cut into contemporary styles and we therefore had to work around this. The hair was styled by Toni Tatlow for P.Kai, Peterborough, proving that if you don't want to wear false hair, you can still create period styles. However, Turbans are also a simple way of hiding short or modern hair.

MAKE-UP

> The French ladies most of them for what I can perceive maybe very beautiful but they dress themselves in a new face everyday.
>
> *The Earl Orrery*[16]

With modern make-up, it is much easier to achieve the perfect Georgian face as described by Sir Henry Beaumont in his book *A Dialogue on Beauty* from 1752:

> The forehead should be white, smooth and open. The skin in general should be white, properly tinged with red with apparent softness and a look of thriving health in it. The cheeks should not be wide; should have a degree of plumpness, with the red and white finely blended together. The eyebrows should be well divided, rather full than thin, semi-circular broader in the middle than at the

ends. The mouth should be small, and the lips not of equal thickness. A truly pretty mouth is like a Rose-bud that is beginning to grow.[17]

However, it was much more complex in the eighteenth century. Faces could also be marked by smallpox, and disfigurement by venereal disease, such as syphilis, could be horrific. Too much sugar meant the rich often lost teeth, which could leave them with sunken cheeks, and too much drink could leave you with red patches where these were not desirable.

However, if you had the money, you could buy all sorts of things to improve your appearance. A white powdered face was fashionable, but most powders contained lead and mercury, which could prove lethal. Patches – small black silk shapes worn on white powdered faces – often covered the signs of early syphilis. This had its own language based on where on the face you placed them. Sunken cheeks could be addressed with cheek plumpers made of leather or cork, or you could buy teeth from those desperate enough to have their healthy teeth pulled out for money and have them transplanted. Those with thin eyebrows need not worry; you could buy mouse skins to wear over your own!

JEWELLERY

> Mrs. Hurst, principally occupied in playing with her bracelets and rings.
>
> *Pride and Prejudice, Jane Austen*[18]

Jewelled flowers and feathers dominated the first half of the century, although miniatures were also worn. After 1758 and the appearance of Halley's Comet, stylized comets became quite a fad, worn on a bodice, sleeves or in the hair. Brooches worn on the bodice could be large, covering the whole stomacher. Three matching brooches in descending size order were also popular and worn on stomachers. Brooches were often used to pin up the skirts of long court dresses, and this is a pretty good solution to handling trains or long skirts on dresses if you plan to

Korina and Kitt model the *robe à l'anglaise*.

dance. Brooches can also be worn as hair ornaments.

Chatelaines – devices that allowed women to attach items such as a watch, keys or pair of scissors to a belt – were worn from the start of our timeline up until the beginning of the nineteenth century.

Diamonds from the new Brazilian diamond mines were worn as they were, and also set on coloured foils to give them a range of fashionable soft pastel hues. Fake or paste diamonds, made from glass, were invented in 1670 by George Ravenscroft in London, who was appointed jeweller to Louis XV in 1734. They were very fashionable as so much more could be done with paste than with real diamonds. Smaller precious stones were set into buttons. Shoe buckles could be heavily jewelled. Cut steel beads and sequins were used throughout this period to give a much less expensive sparkle.

Necklaces were worn throughout the period, often more than one in different lengths. In the 1760s necklaces started to be worn very high on the neck.

Festoon necklaces – many strings of jewels and pendants hanging in one piece, filling in the neckline above the bodice – were very fashionable between 1770 and 1780, following a fashion set by Marie Antoinette.

In revolutionary France, as jewellery could mark you out for the guillotine, the only items worn were symbolic pieces. These would often be bits of stone or metal from the Bastille, iron rings with patriotic mottos and tricolour ribbons. Following the Proclamation of the Empire in 1804, luxury cameos returned and were key to the future of the neoclassical style being worn everywhere. Everything had a classical feel; garlands of gold laurel leaves and simple abstract patterns were common. Matching sets

were popular, with a necklace, bracelets, pendant earrings and hair ornaments, which would consist of items such as tiaras and hair combs. Tiaras were particularly popular around 1800, whilst by 1810 hair combs had taken over.

Pearls, both real and fake, were worn throughout the period, often as a set consisting of necklace, earrings and hairpieces. In 1815 tiny seed pearls became fashionable and were threaded onto horsehair to create delicate lace-like patterns. At the end of our timeline there was a fad for wearing mismatching sets of three chunky bracelets or rings all together on one wrist or finger.

Generally the French wore much more jewellery than the English, who would often only wear items such as diamonds at court. It was also not uncommon for these to be hired for the occasion.

Trimmings

Observing his second daughter
employed in trimming a hat, he
suddenly addressed her with, I hope
Mr. Bingley will like it, Lizzy.

Pride and Prejudice, Jane Austen[19]

Unlike most clothes today, Georgian
and Regency dresses where not ready-
made. Items such as hats were dressed
and re-dressed to match different
gowns and occasions. Pins were
frequently used to allow items to be
removed for cleaning, or to keep pace
with changing fashions. Trimming
could also extend the life cycle of an
item, disguising wear and allowing it to
keep pace with changing fashions. A
knot or cluster of ribbons, flowers,
feathers or even jewels was called a
pompon.

RIBBONS

Ribbons had both practical and
decorative uses. The fashion for
decorative ribbons and bows is a key
look of the Georgian period and this
continued to the end of the century.

Ribbons were popular 'fairings', that
is gifts brought at local fairs, and were
often given as courtship presents. A
contemporary rhyme commemorates
this practice:

He promis'd to bring me a bunch of
blue ribbons,
To tie up my bonny brown hair.

'O Dear! What can the matter be?'

The *robe à l'anglaise* could be a practical and colourful outfit when made up in printed cottons.

PART TWO

Chapter 6 – Project 1: Early Mantua and Masquerade Costume, 1715

NOTES ON PATTERN MARKINGS

The patterns are shown the right way up and in order of stitiching. The centre back lines up to the left-hand side of the page and the centre front lines up to the the right-hand side of the page: for example, the sleeves are all laid out with the back of the sleeve on the left and the front on the right. It is best to add your own markings and notches to the pattern when you scale them up.

Key to pattern markings

CB	centre back of garment
CF	centre front of garment
Solid line inside pattern outline	gather or pleat here
Double-ended arrow	grainline, match to straight grain of fabric
Double-ended arrow pointing to pattern edge	cut on the fold, placing this edge along the fold
Double line inside pattern outline, on stay patterns	boning channel placement
Solid line inside pattern outline ending with a notch	leave open to notch

Mr Addison[1]

Early Mantua

This is a formal court or evening dress, made up of a bodice with train and underskirt, that was first worn in about 1690. It became fashionable across Europe, being popular in England through the 1720s and 1730s. Pinning up the 'tails' of the train was considered a fine art. Only affluent woman would have been able to afford this dress as it is made from silks and satins.

This dress would have been worn with a crisp white linen shift with frills on show at the cuff and neckline. Underneath the dress are long stays without boning across the bust line with a standard width petticoat under the underskirt to keep the shape. You can find the patterns for the shift, stays and petticoat in Chapter 16.

The height of the headdress worn with this dress, which was called a fontange, was a key part of the fashionable look at this time. Should you wish to carry things with you, you could wear pockets; just remember to add slits in your underskirt so you can access them. Rachel also wears lace gloves. See Chapter 5 for more information on other suitable accessories. You can find the patterns for the fontange and pockets in Chapter 16.

What You Will Need

The following will give you an estimate of what you will need. However, as fabric widths vary and patterns may be resized, you should double-check how much fabric you need once you have drawn up your pattern.

Left: Rachel in an early mantua gown.

Fabrics: **Dress:** Between 6.5 and 8.5 metres depending on the width of the fabric, but it is best to check once you have scaled up your pattern.

Underskirt: You will need to cut between two and three panels depending on the fabric width and your personal preference. See Chapter 16 for more information.

Other: Ribbon for lacing or lacing tape; cord for the underskirt; interfacing for the stomacher.

The Bodice

The following instructions are for making the bodice and train with a lining but leaving the sleeves unlined. If you don't want to line the bodice or train, you will need to finish the raw edges of the seams and all other edges at each stage. If you wish to line the sleeves, you can use the same pattern and add sleeves to your bodice lining as described for the outer sleeves.

1. Stitch the bodice back tops together.

2. Next stitch the bodice pieces together, starting from the centre back of the bodice and working outwards to the front, matching any notches as you go and pressing when complete. Leave the shoulder seams unstitched at this stage.

3. On your bodice back tops, press under the seam allowances along the bottom and side edges.

4. Matching centre back to centre back, pin the bodice back top to the bodice back. Once it is lined up, topstitch together and press.

5. Next stitch the shoulder seams together and press. Your bodice should now be complete and at this stage you are ready for a fitting.

The front of the gown.

The back of the gown, showing the tails pinned up.

Make up the bodice lining in the same way.

The Sleeves

1. Stitch each sleeve together, then finish the raw edges and press.

2. Now fit the sleeves into the bodice. I like to have the sleeve with the right side facing, and fit it into the bodice with the bodice on the outside. However you do it, ensure that you are putting the right sides of the sleeve and bodice together and double-check before stitching.

3. Start at the bottom (the underarm) and work up to the top. When you get to the section of the sleeve that is marked on the pattern, pin-tuck or gather the extra fullness into the sleeve hole, making sure both sides match.

4. When you are happy with the way your sleeve looks, stitch it onto the bodice. It is well worth taking the time to get this right.

5. Finish the sleeves by stitching on the cuff. You can stitch the bottom edges, right sides together, and press it up, pressing the raw edges inwards. Hand-stitch to finish.

The side of the gown.

A detail of the front of the bodice.

Front Lacing

Pin loops of ribbon, cord or whatever you plan to use for the front lacing down the centre fronts facing towards the side seams, with spacing to suit the size of the cord or ribbon that you plan to use as lacing. These loops will be stitched in with the lining, but you should also overstitch them now to reinforce them.

LAYPLAN IDEAS

As the train piece is quite large, if you needed to you could cut it in more than one piece. As fabric was so valuable, originals in museums show they were often patched together in this way. This could save you money or enable you to use narrower widths of cloth. If cutting the train in one piece, you may find it best to lay it on a single width of cloth fitting the smaller pieces round it. Remember the pattern pieces will need to be turned over before you cut the second parts!

TRICKY TRAINS

If you worry about wearing pins in your train, try poppers instead. They are much less likely to damage the fabric if they get caught, simply coming undone. If you think it is highly likely that someone will stand on your train, pin the train tails up so they don't touch the floor, just as they would have done in the eighteenth century.

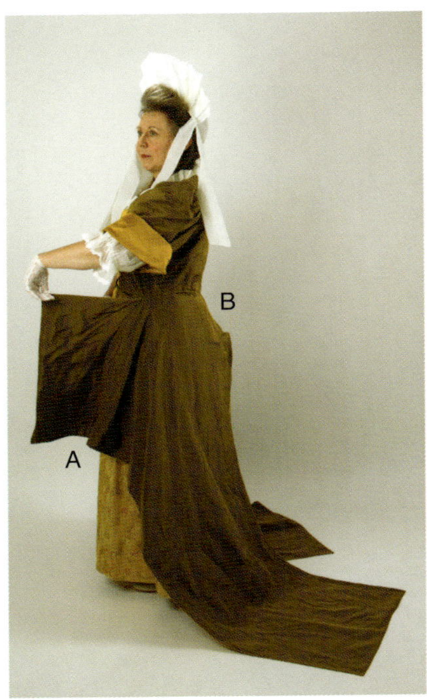

The tails unpinned: pin A to B, folding the tails in half and gathering up the top to complete.

The Train

1. Pin the outer and lining pieces together, with the right sides together, and stitch around the edge, leaving the gap marked on the pattern. This is where your train attaches to the bodice.

2. At this stage, pin both the train pieces to the dress with the right sides together, and then stitch the train to the bodice.

3. Mitre the corners and trim down the seam allowances, before turning the right way round and gently pushing out the corners. Do this with both sides and then press.

Lining the Bodice

Lining the bodice will cover up all the raw edges. If you wish to line your bodice, it should be attached at this stage.

1. Pin the outer and lining pieces together with the right sides together and stitch around the edge, leaving a gap where the train is. This will allow you to turn it the right side out.

2. Mitre the corners and trim down the seam allowances before turning the bodice the right side out. Gently push out the corners and curves before pressing.

3. Next tuck the raw edges inward and stitch the lining over the gap and sleeve holes. Ideally, stitch this by hand. If you prefer, you can use bias binding for the sleeve holes.

The Stomacher

1. Matching the right sides together and with a layer of interfacing on the outside, stitch all the way around, leaving a gap of about 5cm on a straight edge.

2. Mitre the corners and trim down the seam allowances.

3. Turn the stomacher the right side out, gently pushing out the corners and curves.

4. Then press and hand-stitch the gap closed.

Pinning up the Tails

These tails look quite complex when pinned up, but this is simple once you know how. You should only need one pin each side, matching A to B, as marked on the pattern and pinning them together to complete.

The Underskirt

This skirt is made in just the same way as a petticoat.

1. Start by stitching the panels together and finish any raw edges.

2. Turn the top of the skirt over twice, making sure you have enough room to thread your drawstring through the casing you have just made. Stitch through the bottom edge of the turning, catching all of the layers.

3. Make a hole by unpicking one of the the vertical seams on the inside of the skirt above the horizontal stitching completed in the last step. Then hand-stitch over the top and bottom of the hole to ensure it doesn't come undone any further.

4. Attach a safely pin to your cord and feed the cord through the casing until it comes back out. Keep the cord tied to stop it coming out when the skirt is not worn.

5. Mark the correct length for your skirt, turn over the hem allowance twice and stitch.

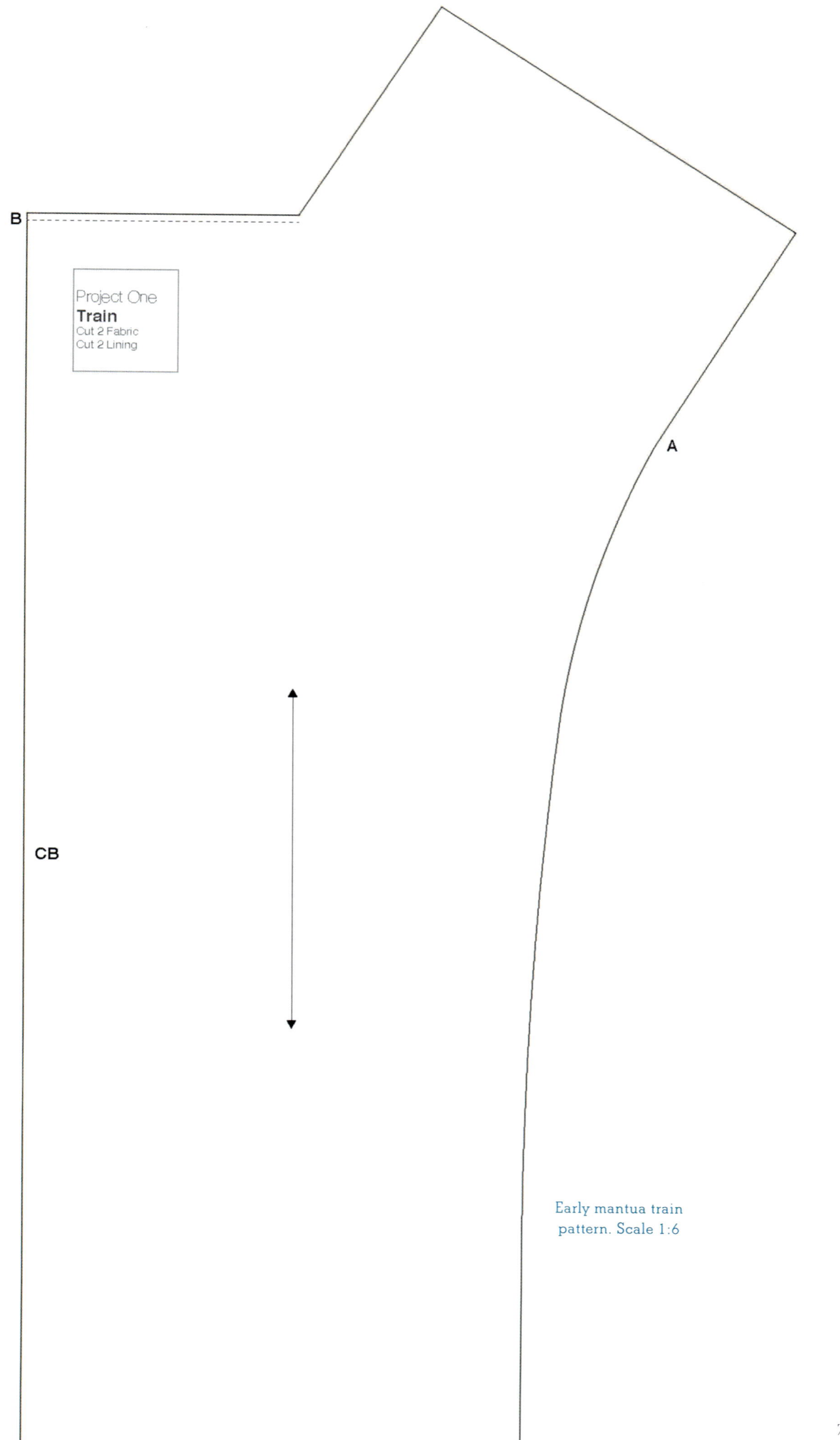

Early mantua train
pattern. Scale 1:6

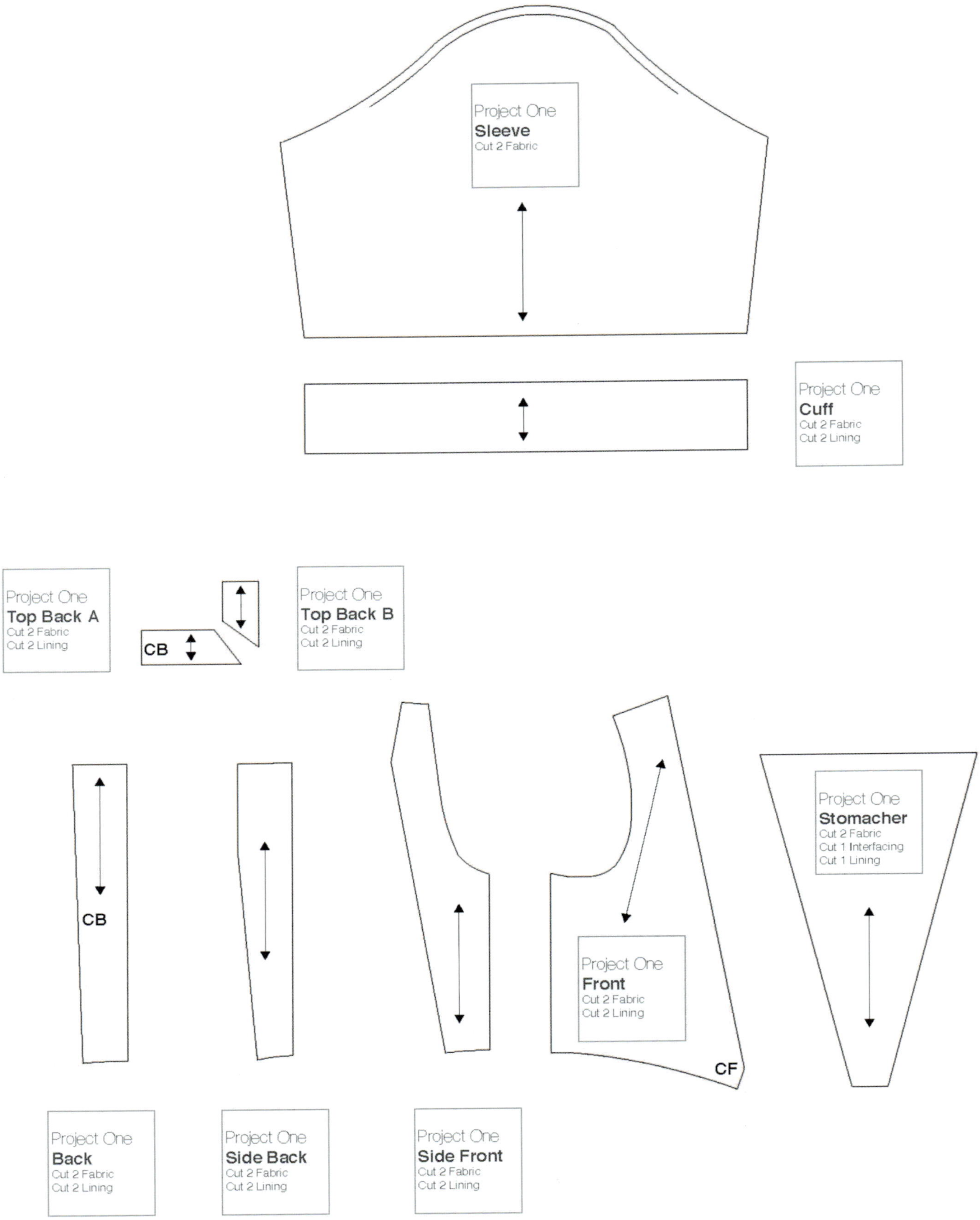

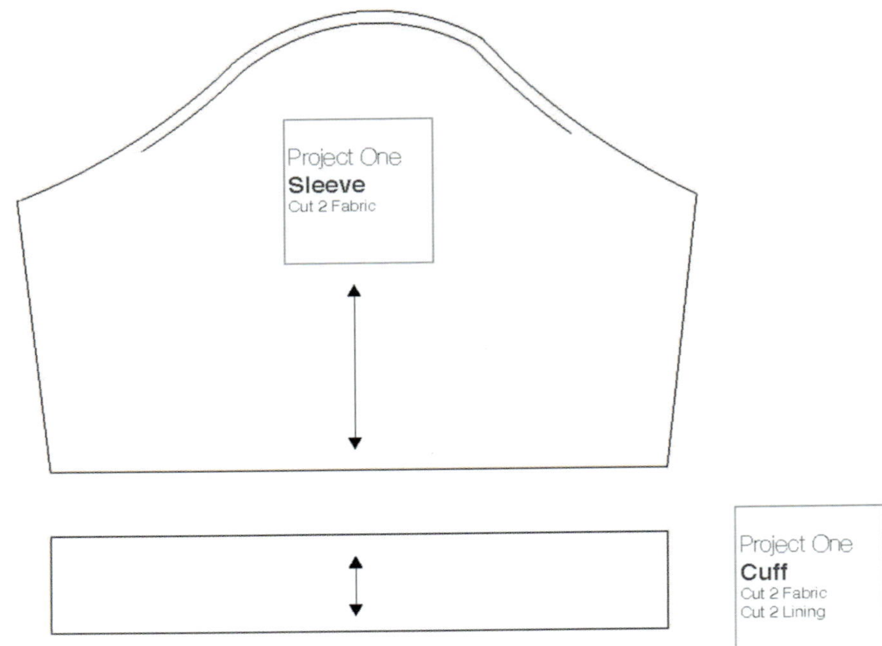

Early Mantua bodice pattern. Scale 1:6

Rachel dressed in a domino cape.

Rachel in masquerade costume.

The Early Mantua Dressed as a Masquerade Costume

Do you know me? Who are you? I know you!

Customary masquerade greeting

Rachel wears a domino, a large full black cape that disguises your true identity under layers of voluminous satin or silk.

The aim was to disguise your identity until the stroke of midnight when everyone was revealed. The quote at the start of this chapter was a customary enquiry between guests at a masquerade ball, which were enormously popular throughout the eighteenth and into the nineteenth centuries.

Rachel's costume is made up of a hooded cape and a mask. Any of the costumes in this book could be period domino costumes if covered with a cape and mask as shown. You may even wish to add a tricorn hat, like that worn with the riding costume in Project 5, or make a black stomacher and add white pom-poms for spots.

What You Will Need

Should you wish to make your own; the pattern for the cape can be found in Chapter 16. Our mask is made out of card, and was bought cheaply from an art shop.

FANCY DRESS

Historical costumes were a popular theme for eighteenth-century masquerades. However, the period shape of contemporary fashionable dress was used and a historical look was built around this structure. If you wish, you could adapt any of the patterns in this book to make your own costume for a historical figure.

Chapter 7 – Project 2: *Robe Volante* and Caraco Jacket, 1730

I find them indecent and will not allow them in my presence. They look as if one was just going to bed.

Madame Duchesse D'Orleans[1]

Robe Volante

Alison wears a striped silk *volante*. To have an informal gown in such fabrics would have required a good deal of disposable income. It would have been worn to greet visitors at home, before more formal dress was required.

This style of dress became fashionable in France after about 1715 and continued to be worn into the 1730s. The design came about from the relaxation of court rules during the reign of the child king Louis XIV and the lack of formal court events associated with this period. This then survived as a style of informal dress or *negligée* after the king came to maturity.

The sleeve worn with this style of cuff is called a pagoda sleeve and was popular throughout the 1730s. It can, however, be applied to any of the costumes with close-fitting sleeves mentioned in this book.

As well as being suitable for informal wear, this style of dress is perfect for the later stages of pregnancy or for anyone who dislikes close-fitting clothing or wearing stays. Should you want the dress to be closer fitting, then you can add lacing to the inside of the centre back of the gown to draw it in more around the bodice.

Paintings from this time show that although the gown was loose, stays were often worn underneath. As well as side hoops and a coif cap to cover her hair, Alison wears a shift and long stays under her gown. You can find the patterns for the shift and stays in Chapter 16.

Alison may also have worn mitts at home to keep her hands warm. See Chapter 5 for more information on other suitable accessories.

What You Will Need

The following will give you an estimate of what you will need. However, as fabric widths vary and patterns may be resized, you should double-check how much fabric you need once you have drawn up your pattern.

Fabrics: Between 8 to 10 metres, depending on the width of the fabric, but it is best to check once you have scaled up your pattern.

Other: Ribbon for lacing or lacing tape.

The Gown

1. Start by stitching together the front and back panels if needed.

2. Next, stitch the gown together at the centre back. Finish the raw edges and press.

3. Now pin the pleats in the back and front panels as marked on the pattern. Once they are pinned correctly, stitch across the top and stay the pleats if needed. You can work out if you need to do this on your toile before making your final gown.

4. If you wish to lace the centre back for a closer fit, add the lacing tape, or make lacing loops with ribbon and hand-stitch these to the inside of the dress down the centre back.

5. Next stitch up the side panels, leaving open the corner marked on the pattern. It is best to finish the raw edges of the side seams before stitching them in order to make pinning and stitching the corner pleats simpler.

6. Now turn the raw edge inwards and then pin the pleats towards the bodice side. When you are finished, the two side seams should line up with no gap.

7. Next hand-tack the pleats in place, working in a circular fashion around from the front to the back or vice versa. Use a running stitch, but try to let as little of your stitching as possible show on the outside, as you do with a slip stitch. If possible, finish by pressing on a curved surface.

8. Now stitch, finish and press the centre front seams

9. Finally, stitch the shoulder panel firstly to the centre back then to the front of the gown, before finishing and pressing.

The Sleeves

1. Stitch each sleeve together, then finish the raw edges and press.

2. Now fit the sleeve into the bodice. I like to have the sleeve with the right side facing, and fit it into the bodice with the bodice on the

The front of the gown.

The back of the gown.

outside. However you do it, ensure you are putting the right sides of the sleeve and bodice together and double-check before stitching.

3. Start at the bottom (the underarm) and work up to the top. When you get to the section of the sleeve that is marked on the pattern, pin-tuck or gather the extra fullness into the sleeve hole, making sure both sides match.

4. When you are happy with the way your sleeve looks, stitch it onto the bodice. It is well worth taking the time to get this right.

The Cuffs

1. Mark, press and stitch the pleats marked on the pattern for both cuffs.

2. Stitch, finish and press the seams.

3. Turn over the bottom and top edges of the cuffs twice and stitch. Your cuffs are now ready to be stitched to your sleeves.

4. Find the centre front of the cuff by folding it and marking the middle distance between the seams with a pin. Match the centre front of the cuff to the notch on the sleeve.

5. Check you are happy with how the cuff is sitting on the sleeve and adjust if needed, before stitching the cuff to the sleeve with a running stitch or similar. You may also want to stitch the top of the cuff to the sleeve seam to stop it drooping.

The side of the gown.

WAYS TO WEAR YOUR *ROBE VOLANTE*

This dress can be worn in different ways. Alison wears her *volante* with side hoops (1730s), but it could also be worn with round hoops for an earlier (1720s) look, or without hoops for a more informal look. If you don't want to wear stays with your *volante*, make up a stomacher from one of the other projects to wear in the centre front.

Finishing Touches

1. To finish the neckline, turn the raw edge in twice and finish by hand-stitching.

2. Lastly, to finish the hem, determine the correct length of the skirt, then turn up the bottom edge of the skirt twice and stitch.

Robe Volante Cut as a Caraco Jacket

> Even the poorest of them, is careful to be in fashion.
>
> *Moritz, German traveller*[2]

Kelly wears a Caraco jacket with simple skirt and matching stomacher. She is dressed as a working-class Georgian, but still as a woman of some means who can afford the latest printed fabrics and silk ribbons.

Caraco jackets were worn by working-class women for everyday activities and by wealthy women at home. The jackets changed very little over the eighteenth century, and from the 1740s onwards it was common for Caraco jackets to be cut with a sack back.

Kelly's outfit is worn over a shift, long stays and a petticoat; you can find the patterns for these in Chapter 16. Kelly is dressed to go to market and accessorize her outfit with a straw hat and shopping basket. Working women would also wear a neckerchief. See Chapter 5 for more information on other suitable accessories.

Kelly is ready for the market.

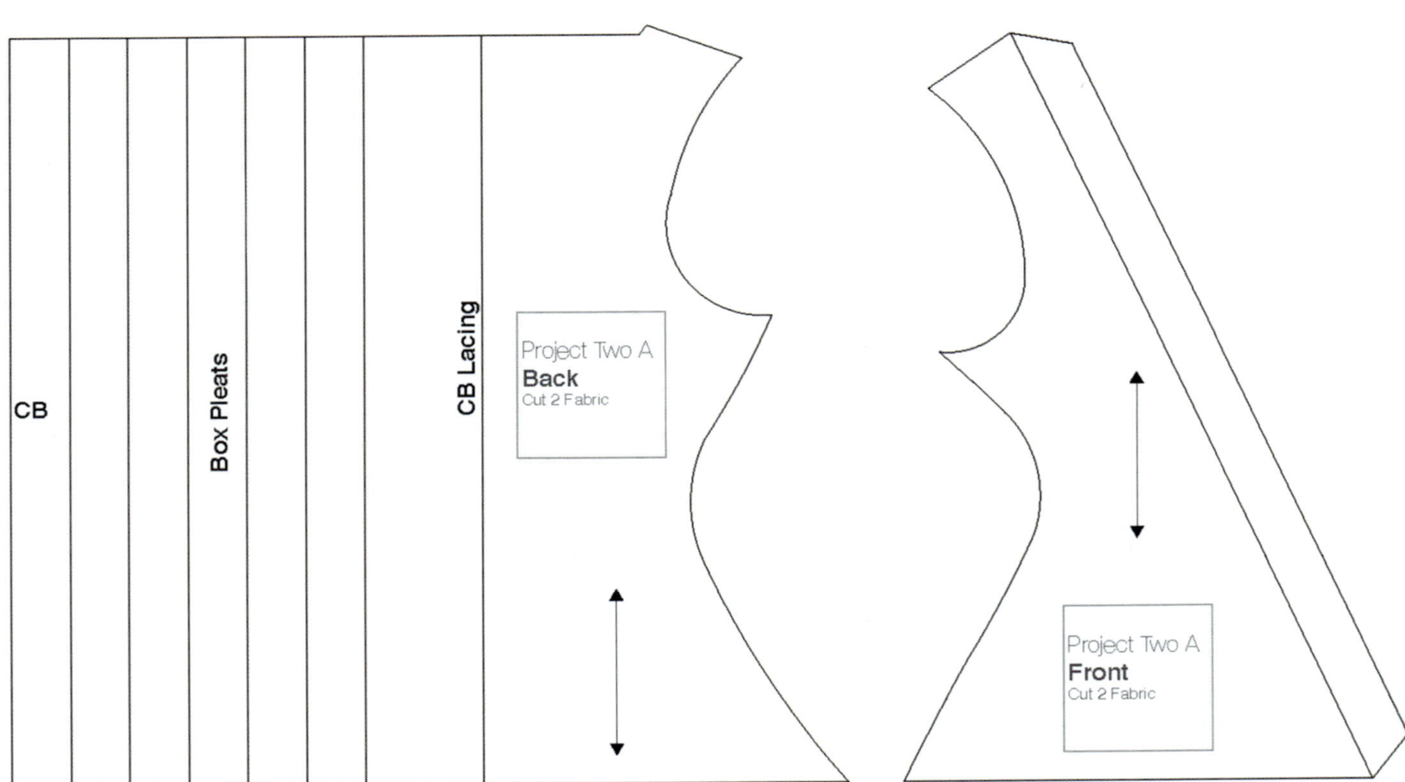

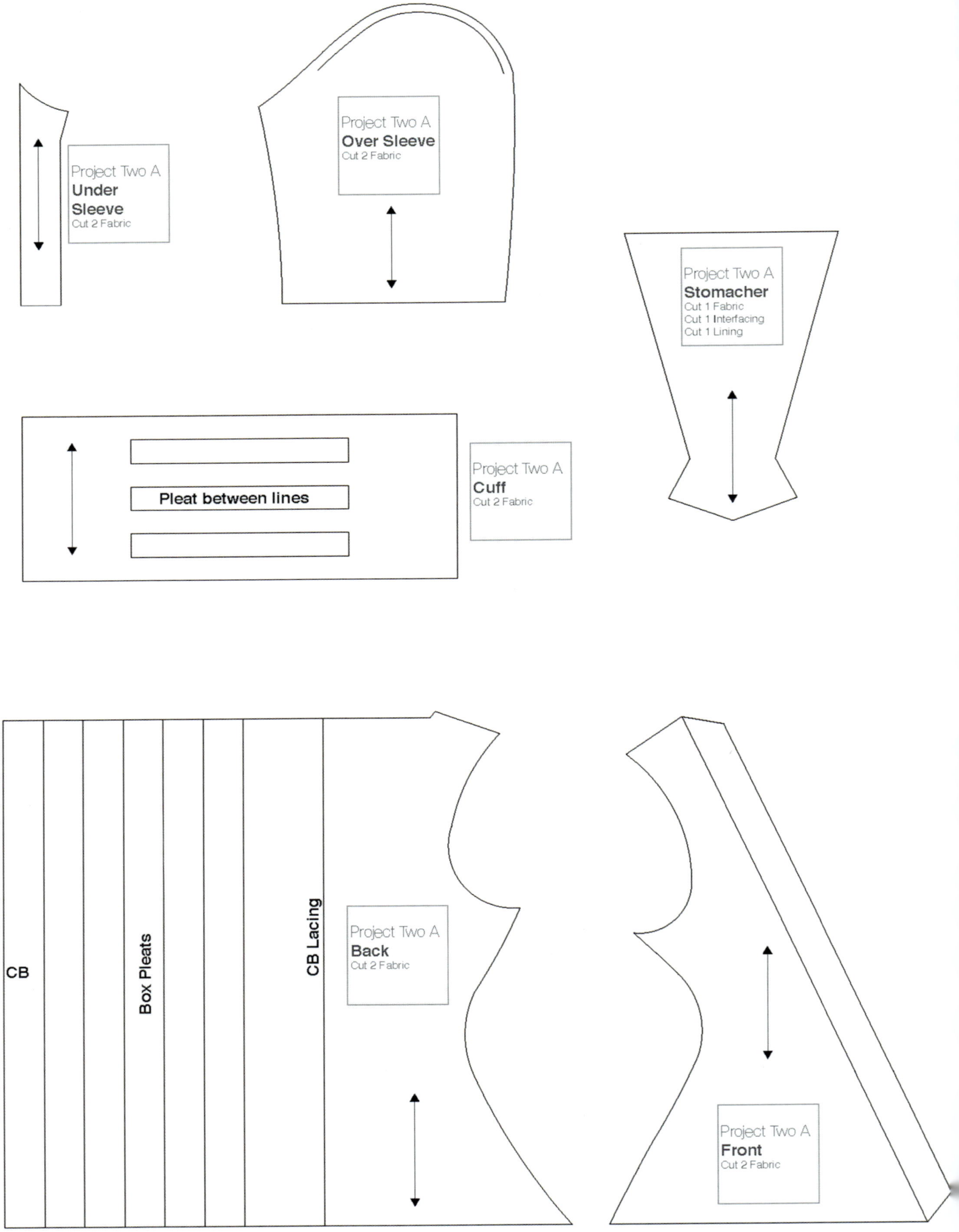

Pattern for Caraco Jacket. Scale 1:6

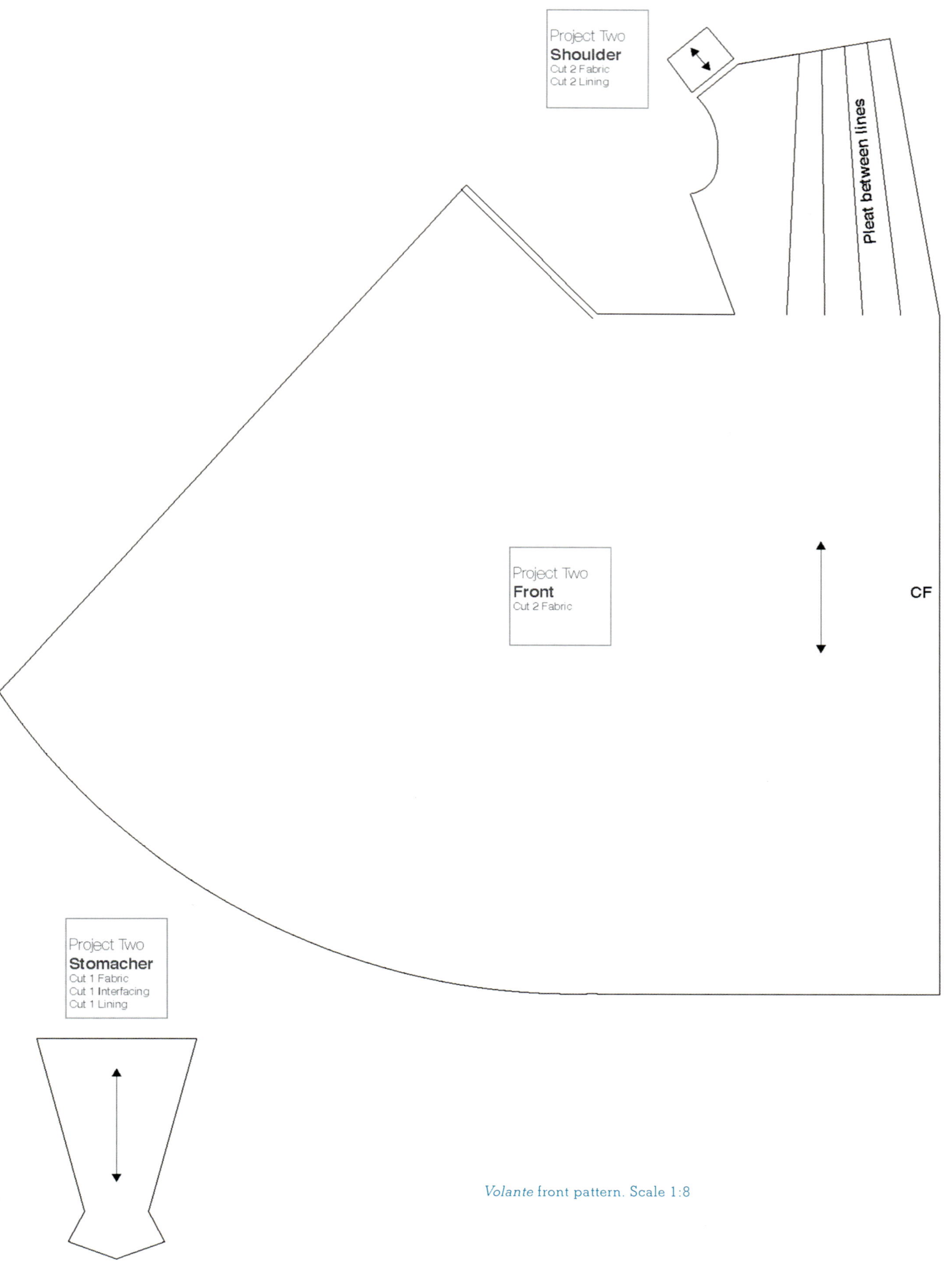

Volante front pattern. Scale 1:8

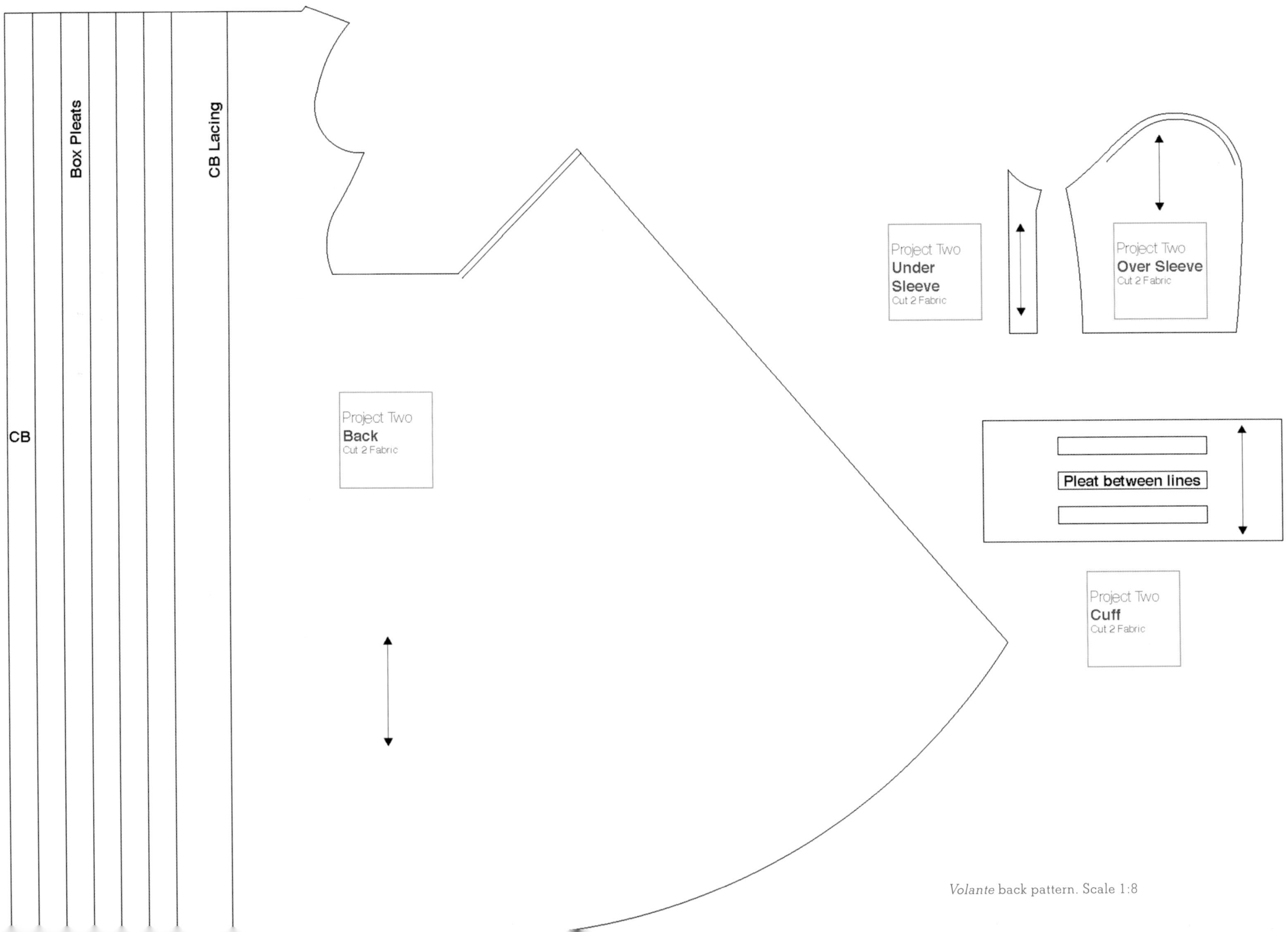

Volante back pattern. Scale 1:8

What You Will Need

The following will give you an estimate of what you will need. However, as fabric widths vary and patterns may be resized, you should double-check how much fabric you need once you have drawn up your pattern.

Fabrics: Jacket: Between 3 and 5 metres, depending on the width of the fabric, but it is best to check once you have scaled up your pattern.

Skirt: You will need to cut between two and three panels, depending on the fabric width and your personal preference. See Chapter 16 for more information.

Other: Ribbon for front ties, interfacing for the stomacher and front lacings, and cord for the skirt.

Jacket Body

1. Stitch the jacket body together at the centre back. Finish and press.

2. Now pin the pleats in the back and front panels as marked on the pattern. Once they are pinned correctly, stitch across the top and stay the pleats if needed. You can work out if you need to do this on your toile before making your final gown.

3. Next, stitch the jacket body together at the side and shoulder seams, before finishing and pressing.

4. Stitch the facings and interfacing to the outside of the jacket body, mitre the corners and trim down the seam allowances. Then turn the right side out and gently push out the corners, before pressing the raw edge under and hand-stitching to finish.

5. Finish the neckline by turning the raw edge over twice and hand-

The front of the gown.

stitch in place, or apply bias binding.

6. Stitch the front ties to the inside of the jacket. The best way to find the most suitable location for the ties is to pin them onto the jacket whilst it is on the body or a mannequin.

7. Turn up the jacket hem twice and hand-stitch in place.

The Sleeves

1. Stitch each sleeve together, then finish the raw edges and press.

2. Now fit the sleeve into the jacket body. I like to have the sleeve with the right side facing, and fit it into the jacket body with the jacket body on the outside. However you do it, ensure you are putting the right sides of the sleeve and jacket

stitched to your sleeves.

4. Check you are happy with how the cuff is sitting on the sleeve and adjust, before stitching the cuff to the sleeve with a running stitch or similar. You may also want to stitch the top of the cuff to the sleeve seams to stop it drooping.

The Stomacher

1. Matching the right sides together and with a layer of interfacing on the outside, stitch all the way around, leaving a gap of about 5cm on a straight edge.

2. Mitre the corners and trim down the seam allowances.

3. Turn the stomacher the right side out, gently pushing out the corners and curves.

4. Then press and hand-stitch the gap closed.

The Skirt
This skirt is made in just the same way as a petticoat.

1. Start by stitching the panels together and finishing any raw edges.

2. Turn the top of the skirt over twice making sure you have enough room to thread your drawstring through the casing you have just made. Stitch through the bottom edge of the turning, catching all of the layers.

3. Make a hole by unpicking one of the vertical seams on the inside of the skirt above the horizontal stitching completed in the last step. Then hand-stitch over the top and bottom of the hole to ensure it doesn't come undone any further.

4. Attach a safely pin to your cord and feed the cord through the

body together and double-check before stitching.

3. Start at the bottom (the underarm) and work up to the top. When you get to the section of the sleeve that is marked on the pattern, pleat it into the sleeve hole, making sure both sides match, the pleats are all going in the same direction and are about the same size.

4. When you are happy with the way your sleeve looks, stitch it onto the jacket body. It is well worth taking

the time to get this right.

The Cuffs

1. Mark, press and stitch the pleats marked on the pattern for both cuffs.

2. Stitch, finish and press the seams.

3. Turn over the bottom and top edges of the cuffs twice and stitch. Your cuffs are now ready to be

casing until it comes back out.
Keep the cord tied to stop it
coming out when not worn.

5. Mark the correct length for your
    skirt, turn over the hem allowance
    twice and stitch.

TRIMMINGS

Ribbons and trims were cheap
ways to dress up clothing for the
working classes; the hems of skirts,
cuffs of sleeves, necklines and front
ties were all perfect for trimming.

The side of the gown.

Chapter 8 – Project 3: *Robe de Cour,* 1740

Robe de Cour

Alison is dressed for court; she wears the *robe de cour,* which was mandatory in the French court and was also worn in England and across Europe. Fashionable from this date and through the 1740s, it was worn in the French court until the 1770s when Louis XVI relaxed the laws and allowed the *robe à la française* to be worn. Large hooped dresses were worn in the English court until the 1820s, although the waistline rose with the fashions.

Such dresses cost a great deal more than most other fashions as the idea was to use them to display your wealth. You would wear the very best that you could afford.

Perhaps the most dramatic and ambitious of all the costumes in this book, this project requires a large amount of fabric and takes some practice if you want to be able to move fluidly in it. Aim to take small steps, as larger steps can make you bounce – you should appear to be a ship sailing serenely on calm waters.

The hoop worn underneath creates the shape of Alison's dress. She also wears a shift, long stays with boning across the bust line, a petticoat, hoops and another petticoat over the hoops. You can find the patterns for these in Chapter 16.

Alison has added accessories to her fine dress. This is achieved by the use of gloves, a fan and ostrich feathers in her hair. See Chapter 5 for more information on other suitable accessories.

What You Will Need

The following will give you an estimate of what you will need. However, as fabric widths vary and patterns may be

Fabrics: Between 7 and 8 metres, depending on the width of the fabric, but it is best to check once you have scaled up your pattern.

Other: Large hooks and eyes, interfacing and cotton tape for the waistband.

The front of the gown.

Left: A detail of the bodice and sleeve.

The back of the gown.

The Sleeves

1. Stitch each sleeve together, then finish the raw edges and press.

2. Now fit the sleeve into the bodice. I like to have the sleeve with the right side facing, and fit it into the bodice with the bodice on the outside. However you do it, ensure you are putting the right sides of the sleeve and bodice together and double-check before stitching.

3. Start at the bottom (the underarm) and work up to the top. When you get to the section of the sleeve that is marked on the pattern, pin-tuck or gather the extra fullness into the sleeve hole, making sure both sides match.

4. When you are happy with the way your sleeve looks, stitch it onto the bodice. It is well worth taking the time to get this right.

The Cuffs

There are two ways to make these frilled cuffs: pinked or lined. The ones illustrated are pinked lace. Instructions for making lined cuffs can be found in Project 4.

1. Using the template on the pattern, trim the edges to shape or trim with pinking shears.

2. Stitch, finish and press the seams.

3. Gather with a running stitch, or pleat in the place marked on the pattern, until the cuff fits the end of the sleeve

4. Turn up the bottom of the sleeves twice and stitch the hem.

5. Line up the cuff seam with the sleeve seam. Check you are happy with how the cuff is sitting on the sleeve and adjust if needed, before stitching the cuff to the sleeve with a running stitch.

resized, you should double-check how much fabric you need once you have drawn up your pattern.

The Bodice

The following instructions are for making the bodice with a lining but leaving the sleeves unlined. If you don't want to line the bodice, you will need to finish the raw edges of the seams and and all other edges at each stage. If you wish to line the sleeves, you can use the same pattern and add sleeves to your bodice lining as

described for the outer sleeves.

1. Stitch the bodice pieces together, starting from the centre back of the bodice and working outwards to the front. Press.

2. Stitch the shoulder seams together, finish and press. At this stage you are ready for a fitting.

Make up the bodice lining in the same way.

The side of the gown.

The Skirt

It is best to fit your skirt over your hoops and petticoat on a stand while you are making it, or alternatively try it on over the hoops to make sure everything sits as it should when it is completed. Firstly, adjust your stand to the right height and dress it in your hoops and petticoat.

1. Start by finishing the raw edges for the top of the skirt.

2. Next, stitch the centre back seam.

3. Then lay the over front skirt on top of the under skirt – the right side of both pieces should face upwards. Now sew the side seams together, sandwiching the under skirt between the skirt back and the over front skirt. Double-check you have all of the right sides facing the same way before stitching, then finish and press.

4. Gather or pin-tuck the fullness as marked on the pattern and turning the skirt the right way round, pin it onto the stand as best you can, leaving the tops open.

5. The next step is to check you are happy with how the front panel sits and how much of the underskirt is on show. You can trim away extra as desired. When you are happy, turn under the edges of the over front skirt twice and finish them.

6. Next you need to adjust the side seams until they sit correctly. Firstly, turn the raw edge inwards and then pin the pleats towards the bodice side. When you are finished, the two side seams should line up with no gap.

7. Then hand-tack the pleats in place, working in a circular fashion around from the front to the back or vice versa. Use a running stitch, but try to let as little of your stitching as possible show on the outside, as you do with a slip stitch. If possible, finish by

Lining the Bodice

Lining the bodice will cover up all the raw edges. If you wish to line your bodice, it should be attached at this stage.

1. Pin the outer and lining pieces together with the right sides together and stitch around the edge, leaving a gap to allow you to turn it the right side out.

2. Mitre the corners and trim down the seam allowances. Turn the bodice the right side out. Gently push out the corners and curves before pressing.

3. Next tuck the raw edges inward and stitch the lining over the gap and sleeve holes. Ideally, stitch this by hand. If you prefer, you can use bias binding for the sleeve holes.

The Stomacher

1. Matching the right sides together and with a layer of interfacing on the outside, stitch all the way around, leaving a gap of about 5cm on a straight edge.

2. Mitre the corners and trim down the seam allowances.

3. Turn the stomacher the right side out, gently pushing out the corners and curves.

4. Then press and hand-stitch the gap closed.

Chapter 16 for skirts and petticoats. You need one length of fabric for an unlined train and two lengths for a lined train. Cut your desired shape at the end that touches the floor; leave the end that attaches to the dress straight. If you have a fabric that will not fray, such as the lace shown on this costume, you do not need finish the edges. You only need to gather or pleat the top and attach it to the costume. Stitch it inside the bottom of the bodice or pin it to the skirt waistband; otherwise you will need to line the train or turn the raw edges over twice and stitch them. If using a lining, cut two pieces. Then with the right sides together, stitch, trim, mitre and turn the right side out before gently pressing out the corners. Then press and continue as before.

TRICKY TRAINS

If you don't want to pin the train to your skirt and you don't want it stitched to your gown, try poppers instead. They are much less likely to damage the fabric if it gets caught, or if someone stands on it. Instead, they will simply just come undone without damaging the train. For dancing, use a brooch to pin your train up out of harm's way.

pressing on a curved surface.

8. Use a pin to mark where the side seams need to be stitched between the waist and the pleats, remembering to leave a gap for pockets if you plan to wear them. You can stitch these seams once the skirt is off the stand.

9. While you have the skirt on the stand, you can pin up the hem ready for stitching.

10. Making sure you have secured everything that isn't yet stitched, remove the skirt from the stand, stitch the front overskirt to the underskirt at the top and the side seams, and then apply a fat cotton tape to the waist on the outside. Stitch the tape to the skirt at the top, leaving space for the tape to be turned inside the skirt, pressed and stitched down to form the waistband. Stitch a hook and eye to the centre back to hold the skirt closed.

11. Finally hem the skirt and underskirt.

The Train

You can create a pattern for a train in the same manner as described in

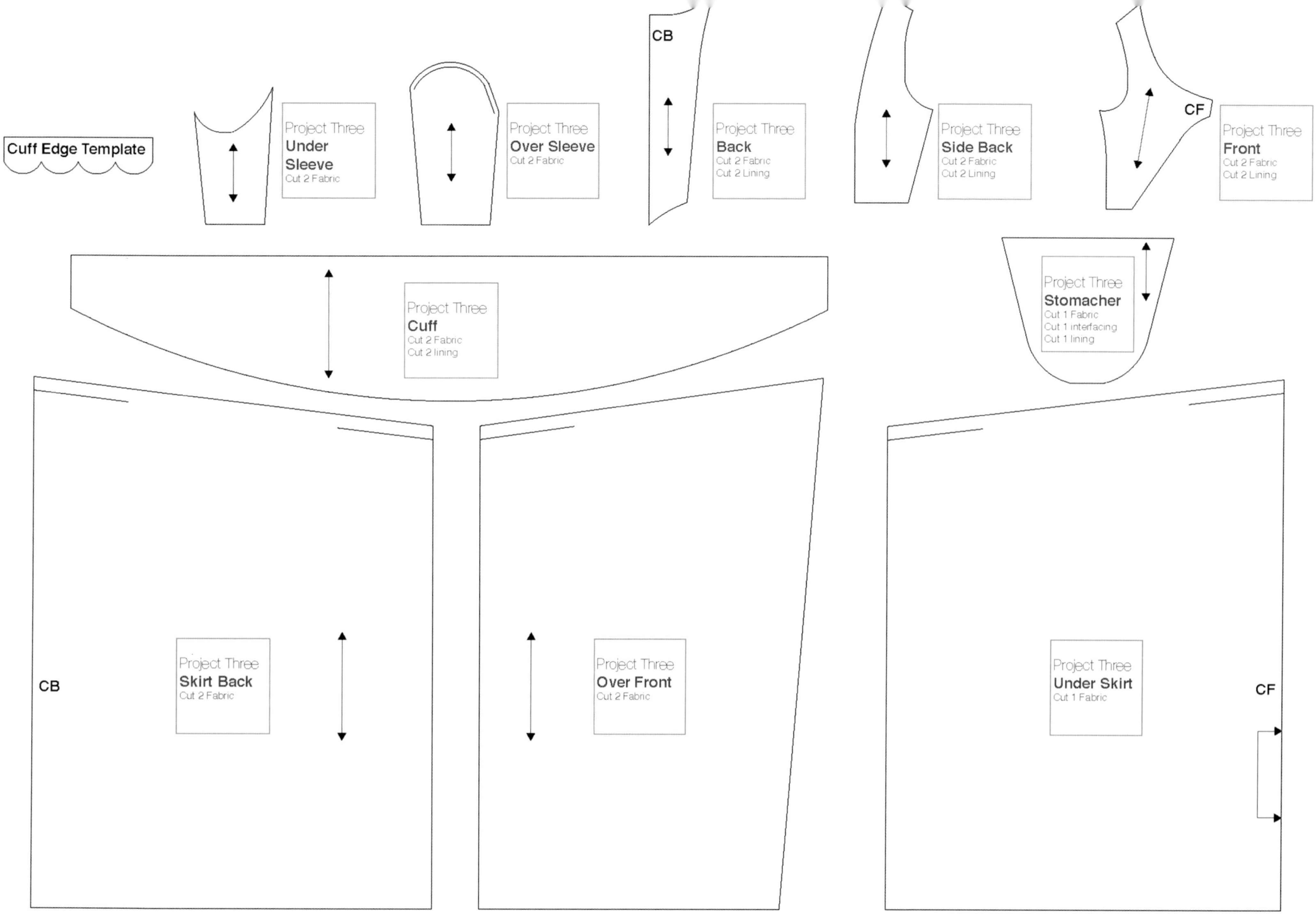

Robe de Cour Pattern. Scale 1:10

Chapter 9 – Project 4: *Robe à la française, 1755*

Robe à la française

Alison wears a *robe à la française*, a gown 'in the French style', often called the sacque or sack by English and American wearers. This is a style that evolved from those that went before it and was worn in one form or another until nearly the end of the 1770s. Early styles had three or four pleats as shown in this costume; later gowns layer the pleats one on top of another, as two double pleats. This pattern can be styled with two or three double pleats. The loose pleats flow over a snug bodice lining to create a style that is both fitted and free-flowing. All women at all levels of society wore these pleats, but only ladies of means could have afforded such a gown made in silk.

Alison wears her gown over a shift, long stays with boning across the bust line, standard petticoat and pocket hoops; you can find the patterns for these in Chapter 16.

Alison accessorises her dress with a fan and gold earrings. See Chapter 5 for more information on other suitable accessories.

What You Will Need

The following will give you an estimate

Fabrics: Between 6 and 7 metres, depending on the width of the fabric, but it is best to check once you have scaled up your pattern.

Other: Ribbon for lacing or lacing tape, cord for the underskirt, interfacing for the stomacher.

of what you will need. However, as fabric widths vary and patterns may be resized, you should double-check how much fabric you need once you have drawn up your pattern.

The Gown

The following instructions are for making the gown with a bodice lining but leaving the sleeves unlined. If you don't want to line the bodice, you will need to finish the raw edges of the seams and all other edges at each stage. If you wish to line the sleeves, you can use the same pattern and add sleeves to your bodice lining as described for the outer sleeves.

1. Stitch the bodice together at the side and side back seams. Leave the centre back and front seams open.

2. Next stitch the shoulder seams together and press.

3. Stitch both sides of the sack back into the centre back bodice seam as marked on the pattern.

4. Next stitch the skirt pieces to the gown from the waist down, finish and press.

5. Turn under the edge of the skirt fronts twice and stitch down.

6. Then pleat the skirt tops to fit the bodice, making sure the pleats all face the same way, are the same size and both sides of the gown match. Before stitching, try the gown over pocket hoops to ensure everything sits right. Once you are happy with the way the pleats look, stitch the skirt to the bodice.

Make up the bodice lining in the same way, starting at the centre back and

working around to the front, which is left open. Stitch the shoulder seams and press.

The Sleeves

1. Stitch each sleeve together, then finish the raw edges and press.

2. Now fit the sleeves into the bodice. I like to have the sleeve with the right side facing, and fit it into the bodice with the bodice on the outside. However you do it, ensure you are putting the right sides of the sleeve and bodice together and double-check before stitching.

3. Start at the bottom (the underarm) and work up to the top. When you get to the section of the sleeve that is marked on the pattern, pin-tuck or gather the extra fullness into the sleeve hole, making sure both sides match.

4. When you are happy with the way your sleeve looks, stitch it onto the bodice. It is well worth taking the time to get this right.

The Cuffs

There are two ways to make these frilled cuffs: pinked or lined. These are lined. Instructions for making pinked cuffs can be found in Project 3.

1. Cut two of each cuff.

2. Stitch up the cuff seam of both the outer fabric and lining fabric and put each set together right side to right side. Then stitch around the decorative hem traced from the pattern, trim and mitre.

3. Next turn each cuff the right way

out and gently push out the corners and curves, before finally pressing and finishing the top edge.

4. Gather with a running stitch or pleat in the place marked on the pattern until the cuff fits over the end of the sleeve

5. Turn up the hem of the sleeves twice and stitch in place.

6. To attach the cuff to the sleeve, line up the cuff seam with the sleeve seam. Check you are happy with how the cuff is sitting on the sleeve and adjust if needed, before stitching the cuff to the sleeve with a running stitch.

The Front Lacing

Pin loops of ribbon, cord or whatever you plan to use for the front lacing down the centre fronts, facing towards the side seams, with spacing to suit the size of the cord or ribbon that you plan to use as lacing. These loops will be stitched in with the lining, but you should also overstitch them now to reinforce them.

To save money and allow you to be able to afford nicer fabric, you can panel your underskirt. Use your fine silk fabric for a front panel of the underskirt and use plain, ideally matching coloured cotton for the parts of the skirt that you can't see.

Lining the Bodice

Lining the bodice will cover up all the raw edges. If you wish to line your bodice, it should be attached at this stage.

1. Pin the outer and lining pieces together with the right sides together and stitch around the

Should you wish for a smoother shape for your gown, try using pads rather than pocket hoops. You can find the pattern for both pocket hoops and pads in Chapter 16.

edge, leaving a gap to allow you to turn it the right side out.

2. Mitre the corners and trim down the seam allowances before turning the bodice the right side out. Gently push out the corners and curves before pressing.

3. Next tuck the raw edges inward and stitch the lining over the gap and sleeve holes. Ideally, stitch this by hand. If you prefer, you can use bias binding for the sleeve holes.

The Stomacher

1. Matching the right sides together and with a layer of interfacing on the outside, stitch all the way around, leaving a gap of about 5cm on a straight edge.

2. Mitre the corners and trim down the seam allowances.

3. Turn the stomacher the right side out, gently pushing out the corners and curves.

The front of the gown.

The side of the gown.

The back of the gown.

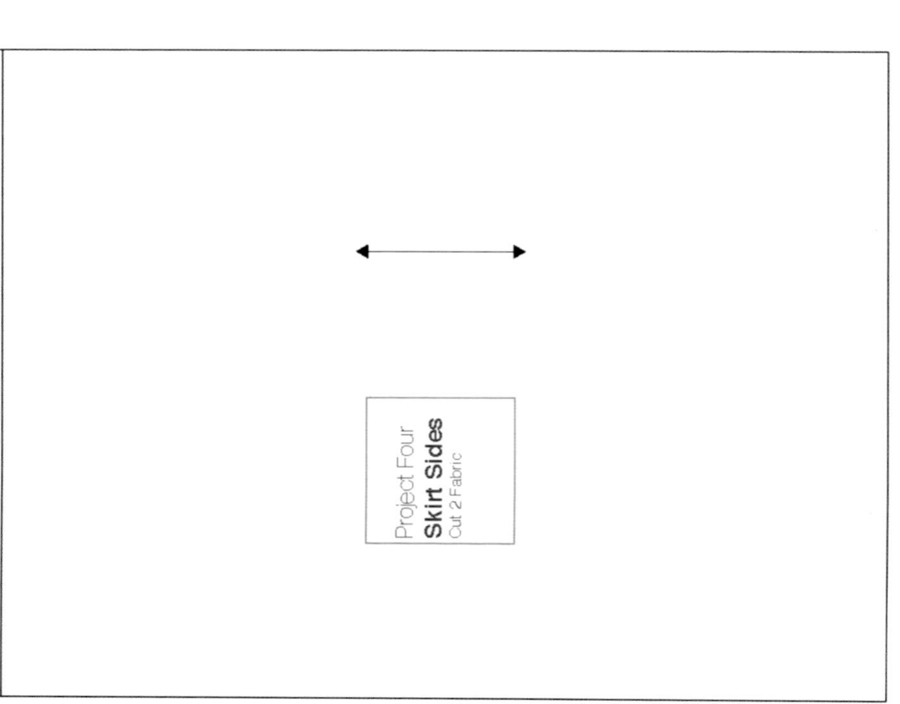

Robe à la française Skirt pattern. Scale 1:8

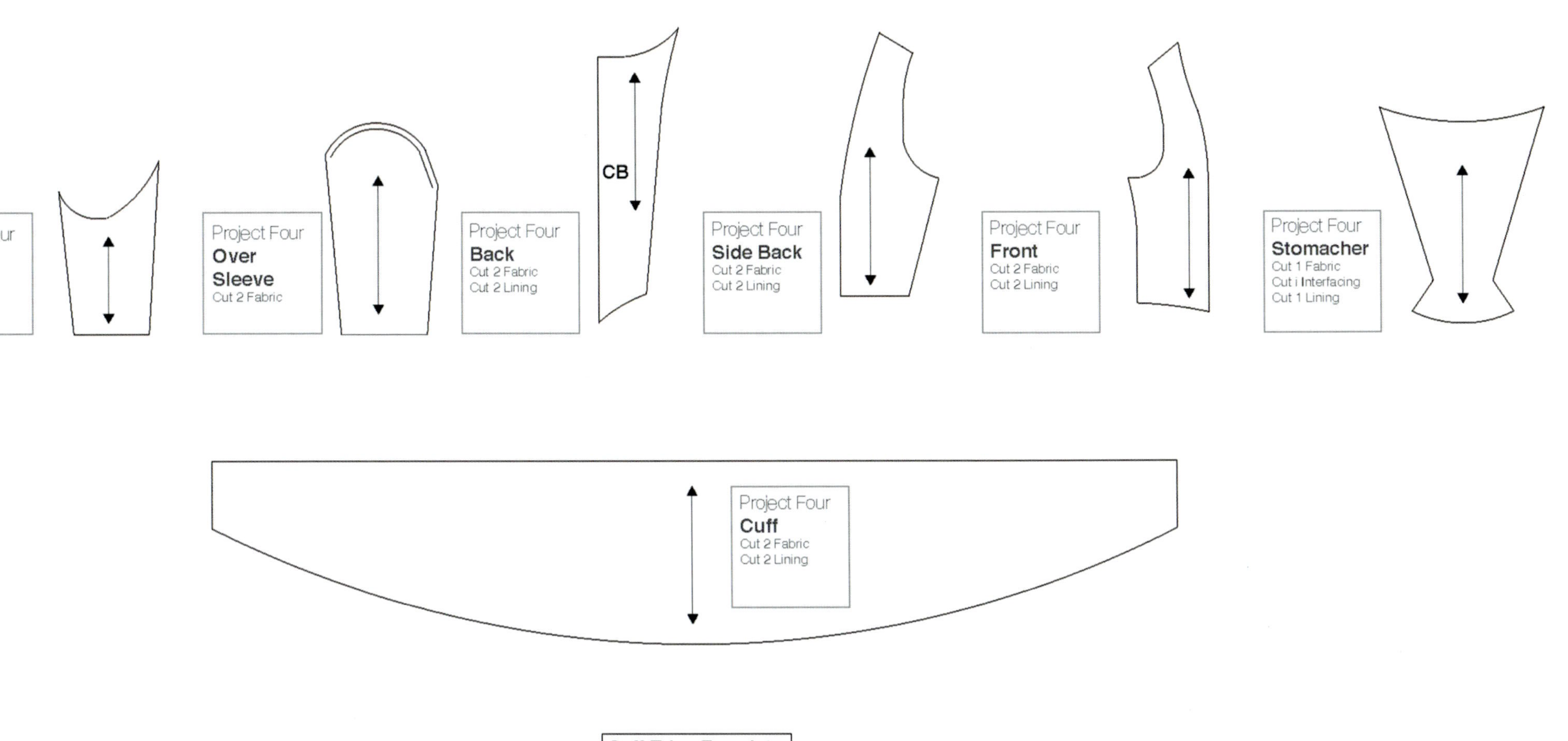

Robe à la française Bodice pattern. Scale 1:8

4. Then press and hand-stitch the gap closed.

The Underskirt

This skirt is made in just the same way as a petticoat.

1. Start by stitching the panels together and finish any raw edges.

2. Turn the top of the skirt over twice, making sure you have enough room to thread your drawstring through the casing you have just made. Stitch through the bottom edge of the turning, catching all of the layers.

3. Make a hole by unpicking one of the vertical seams on the inside of the skirt above the horizontal stitching completed in the last step. Then hand-stitch over the top and bottom of the hole to ensure it doesn't come undone any further.

4. Attach a safely pin to your cord and feed the cord through the casing until it comes back out. Keep the cord tied to stop it coming out when not worn.

5. Mark the correct length for your skirt, turn over the hem allowance twice and stitch.

Chapter 10 – Project 5: *Robe à l'anglaise* and Riding Habit, 1770

10

Never before have women dressed with such simplicity.

le tableau de Paris[1]

Robe à l'anglaise

The model wears a *robe à l'anglaise*, as it is called in French, but it is really just an English-style gown. From the 1770s women started to wear closed gowns, which were really forerunners for the modern concept of a dress. This dress is made from fashionable printed cotton. This fashion was worn as an open gown long before this date in England and became fashionable in France in the 1770s. This costume could have been worn by a working-class woman in England or rich, fashionable French women.

The dress is worn over a shift, long stays with boning across the bust line and a petticoat; you can find the patterns for these in Chapter 16. Although the dress can be worn with smaller pads, it is shown here without them.

Such a simple style needs simple accessories, as the above quote that opens the chapter goes on to say:

A straw hat with a ribbon, kerchief, an apron at home.

The model wears her dress with a kerchief or fichu, gloves and a turban. See Chapter 5 for more information on other suitable accessories.

What You Will Need

The following will give you an estimate of what you will need. However, as fabric widths vary and patterns may be resized, you should double-check how much fabric you need once you have drawn up your pattern.

Fabrics: Between 5 and 6 metres depending on the width of the fabric, but it is best to check once you have scaled up your pattern.

Skirt: You will need to cut between two and three panels depending on the fabric width and your personal preference. See Chapter 16 for more information.

Other: Ribbon for lacing or lacing tape, large hook and eyes.

The Bodice

The following instructions are for making the bodice with a lining but leaving the sleeves unlined. If you don't want to line the bodice, you will need to finish the raw edges of the seams and all other edges at each stage. If you wish to line the sleeves, you can use the same pattern and add sleeves to your bodice lining as described for the outer sleeves.

1. Stitch the bodice together from centre back around to centre front, which should be left open. Finish and press.

2. Next, stitch the shoulder seams together. You are now ready for a fitting.

Make up the bodice lining in the same way.

Back Lacing

1. Turn under the centre front bodice edges twice and stitch.

2. Pin loops of ribbon, cord or whatever you plan to use for the front lacing, down the centre front edges facing towards the side seams, with spacing to suit the size of the cord or ribbon that you plan to use as lacing. Make sure when the bodice is laced there won't be a gap at the back. These loops will be stitched in with the lining, but you should also overstitch them now to reinforce them.

The Sleeves

1. Stitch each sleeve together, leaving a gap at the cuff as marked on the pattern, before finishing the raw edges and pressing.

2. Now fit the sleeves into the bodice. I like to have the sleeve with the right side facing, and fit it into the bodice with the bodice on the outside. However you do it, ensure you are putting the right sides of the sleeve and bodice together and double-check before stitching.

3. Start at the bottom (the underarm) and work up to the top. When you get to the section of the sleeve that is marked on the pattern, pin-tuck or gather the extra fullness into the sleeve hole, making sure both sides match.

4. When you are happy with the way your sleeve looks, stitch it onto the bodice. It is well worth taking the time to get this right.

The Skirt

1. Stitch the side seams together, finishing the edges if needed.

2. Pleat or gather the skirt until it fits

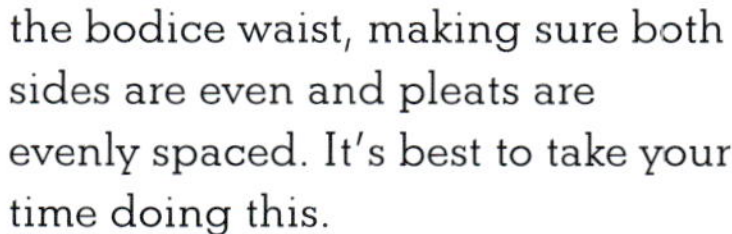
The front of the gown.

The back of the gown.

The side of the gown.

the bodice waist, making sure both sides are even and pleats are evenly spaced. It's best to take your time doing this.

3. When you are happy with the way your pleats look, pin then stitch the skirt to the waist edge of the bodice.

Lining the Bodice

Lining the bodice will cover up all the raw edges. If you wish to line your bodice, the lining should be attached at this stage.

1. Pin the outer and lining pieces together with the right sides together and stitch around the edge, leaving a gap to allow you to turn it the right way out.

2. Mitre the corners and trim down

WAYS TO WEAR YOUR *ROBE À L'ANGLAISE*

You can cut this gown as an earlier open-style gown by making the fastening at the centre front of the gown and using hooks and eyes to close it, as in Project 6. Cut the gown down the centre front to leave a gap each side of the centre front of the bodice to show the underskirt and make an underskirt as described in Project 2.

the seam allowances before turning the bodice the right side out. Gently push out the corners and curves before pressing.

3. Next tuck the raw edges inward and stitch the lining over the gap and sleeve holes. Ideally, stitch this by hand. If you prefer, you can use bias binding for the sleeve holes.

Finishing the Bodice

Hem the bottom edges of the sleeve and the skirt.

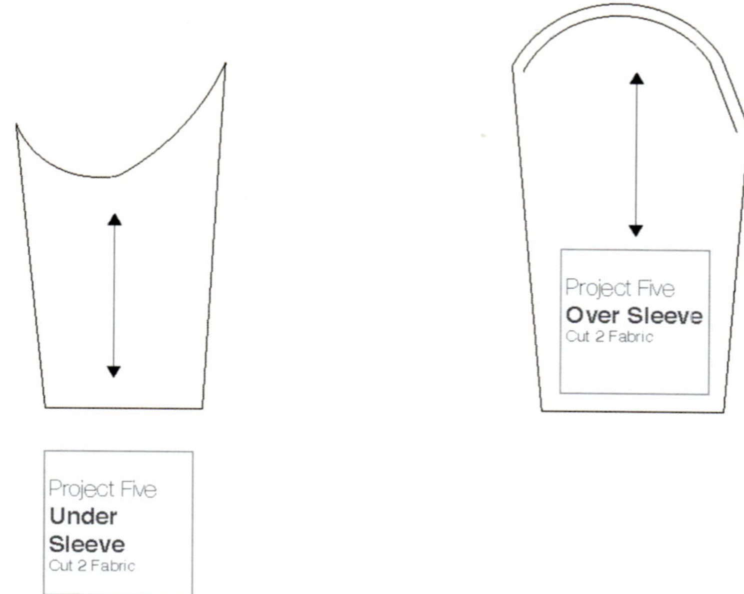

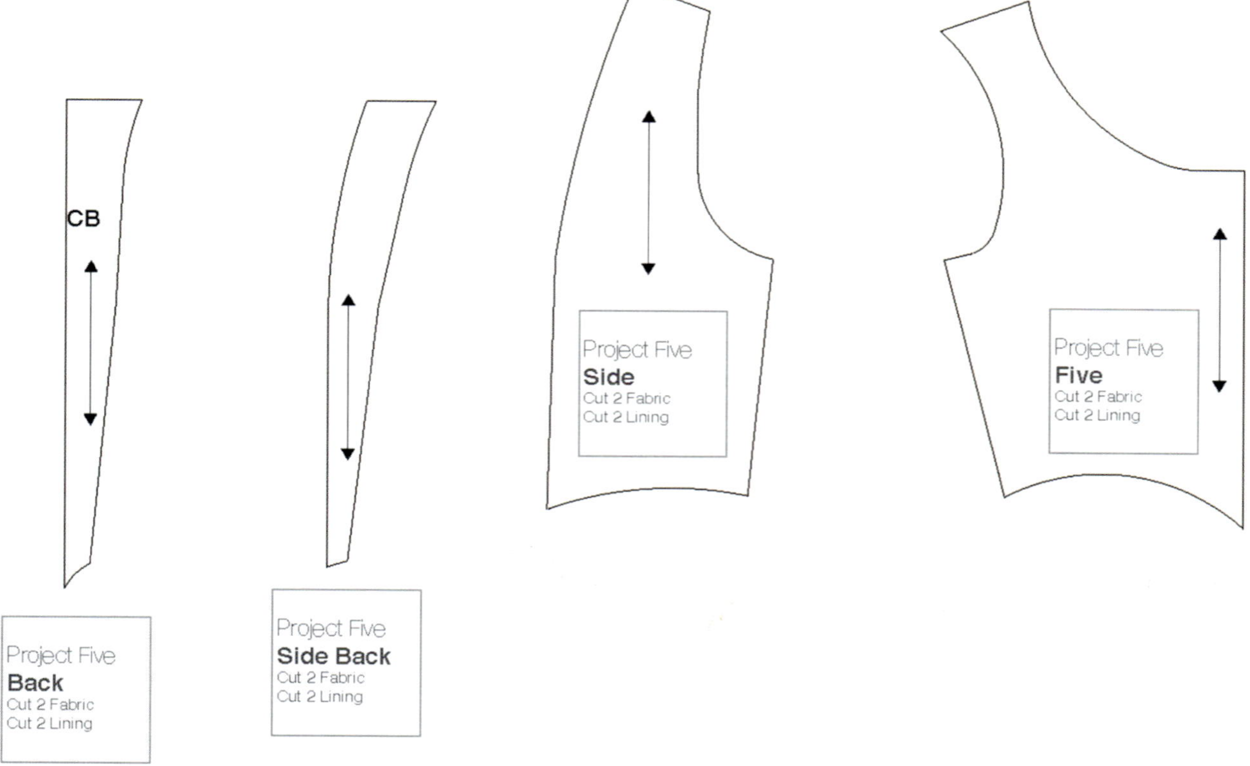

Robe à l'anglaise pattern. Scale 1:6

It is a mixture of the epic with the softness of the ode.

The Guardian, John Gay[2]

The model wears a riding habit, adapted from the *robe à l'anglaise* pattern. This was worn both for riding and also as a travelling dress. Lady Mary Montagu wore hers for travelling in 1717: 'I was in my travelling habit, which is a riding dress.'[3]

It was also acceptable to wear a riding habit as morning dress. Normally made from worsted wool, in England they were made by tailors rather than mantua makers. The jacket was cut in a simpler style to a man's coat. Women with enough money to keep a horse and with the time to ride it, or to travel, wore riding habits. Women wore riding costumes throughout our timeline. This style of dress could be worn up until the time waistlines rose, when the cut of the riding habit followed suit. Although breeches were worn by women in some European countries, riding sidesaddle in a skirt was the norm in England.

The standard underwear of the period, including stays, would have been worn under a riding habit, although hoops and pads are not advised. You can find the patterns for the shifts, stays and petticoats in Chapter 16.

The model's riding habit consists of a skirt and a jacket with boots, a shirt, a waistcoat, a cravat, leather gloves and a tricorn hat. See Chapter 5 for more information on other suitable accessories.

What You Will Need

The following will give you an estimate of what you will need. However, as fabric widths vary and patterns may be resized, you should double-check how much fabric you need once you have drawn up your pattern.

Fabrics: Between 6 and 7 metres, depending on the width of the fabric, but it is best to check once you have scaled up your pattern.

Skirt: You will need to cut between two and three panels depending on the fabric width and your personal preference. See Chapter 16 for more information.

Other: Buttons, trim for the fronts. We have used bias binding, but you could used ribbon or braid.

The Jacket

The following instructions are for making the jacket body with a lining but leaving the sleeves unlined. If you don't want to line the jacket body, you will need to finish the raw edges of the seams and all other edges at each stage. If you wish to line the sleeves, you can use the same pattern and add sleeves to your body lining as described for the outer sleeves.

1. Stitch the jacket body together from centre back to the front, which is left open. Press.

The model, seated in her riding habit.

2. Make up the jacket body lining as above.

3. Next stitch the jacket skirts together from centre back to the centre front, which is left open. Press.

4. Make up jacket skirt lining as above.

5. Stitch the jacket skirt and jacket skirt lining together with the right sides together, stitching around the edge and leaving a gap along the skirt tops to stitch it to the jacket body.

6. Mitre the corners and trim down the seam allowances before turning the jacket skirt the right way out. Gently push out the corners and curves before pressing.

7. On the jacket skirt pin the pleats as marked on the pattern. Stitch along the top of the pleats and press.

8. Stitch the jacket skirt to the jacket body. Press. At this stage you are ready for a fitting.

9. Tuck in the raw edges at the hem and cuffs and stitch the lining over them.

10. Stitch trim to the front of jacket.

11. Stitch hook and eyes to front or buttons if preferred. To work out placement, start with one on the waist and then fit others as needed along the centre front edge.

The Sleeve

1. Stitch cuffs to each sleeve piece.

2. Stitch each sleeve together, finish the raw edges and press.

3. Now fit the sleeves into the jacket bodice. I like to have the sleeve with the right side facing and fit it into the jacket bodice, with the

FASTENINGS

Original eighteenth century gowns fastened at the front until the end of the century when fashions changed and fastenings along with them. Costume designers often move the fastenings, for a wide range of reasons. In this case the gown would have been front fastening and the instructions show how to make it this way, but the example has a back fastening as it was necessary for its intended purpose. If you want to swap from one to the other you only need reverse the words 'front' and 'back' in the instructions.

jacket bodice on the outside. However you do it, ensure you are putting the right sides of the sleeve and jacket bodice together and double-check before stitching.

4. Start at the bottom (the underarm) and work up to the top. The top sleeve seam should be in line with the jacket shoulder seam. When you get to the section of the sleeve that is marked on the pattern, pin-tuck or gather the extra fullness into the sleeve hole, making sure both sides match.

5. When you are happy with the way your sleeve looks, stitch it onto the bodice. It is well worth taking the time to get this right.

The Collar

1. Stitch the collar seams together and press.

2. Then apply interfacing to one side of the collar, using either iron-on or sew-in interfacing.

3. Pin the right sides of the two collar pieces together, then stitch around the sides and top, leaving a gap

The front of the riding habit.

where the collar joins the jacket.

4. Mitre the corners and trim down the seam allowances before turning the collar the right side out. Gently push out the corners and curves before pressing.

5. Stitch the underside of the collar to the jacket neck, matching centre back seams. Press the raw edge under and hand-stitch down.

The Jacket Lining

Lining the jacket will cover up all the raw edges. If you wish to line your jacket, the lining should be attached at

The side of the riding habit.

The back of the riding habit.

this stage.

1. Pin the outer and lining pieces together with the right sides together and stitch around the edge, leaving a gap to allow you to turn it the right side out.

2. Mitre the corners and trim down the seam allowances before turning the bodice the right side out. Gently push out the corners and curves before pressing.

3. Next, tuck the raw edges inward and stitch the lining over the gap and sleeve holes. Ideally, stitch this by hand. If you prefer you, can use bias binding for the sleeve holes.

Finishing the Jacket

1. Hem the bottom edges of the cuffs.

2. Add buttons to the top of the jacket skirt pleats and, if desired, to one side of the jacket centre front.

The Skirt

Use the pattern piece from Project 10 for the skirt waistband.

1. Stitch the skirt seams together and finish the edges if needed.

2. Apply interfacing to the waistband. Fold the waistband in half lengthways and stitch at each end.

3. Mitre the corners and trim down the seam allowances before turning the waistband the right way out. Gently push out the corners before pressing.

4. Pleat or gather the skirt until it fits the waistband, making sure both sides are even and pleats are evenly spaced. It is worth taking your time to ensure that you get this right.

5. Stitch the skirt onto the waistband, then press the raw edge under and hand-stitch in. Add a hook and eye to close the waistband.

6. Hem the skirt to the correct length. Riding habit skirts were often shorter than other skirts for practical reasons.

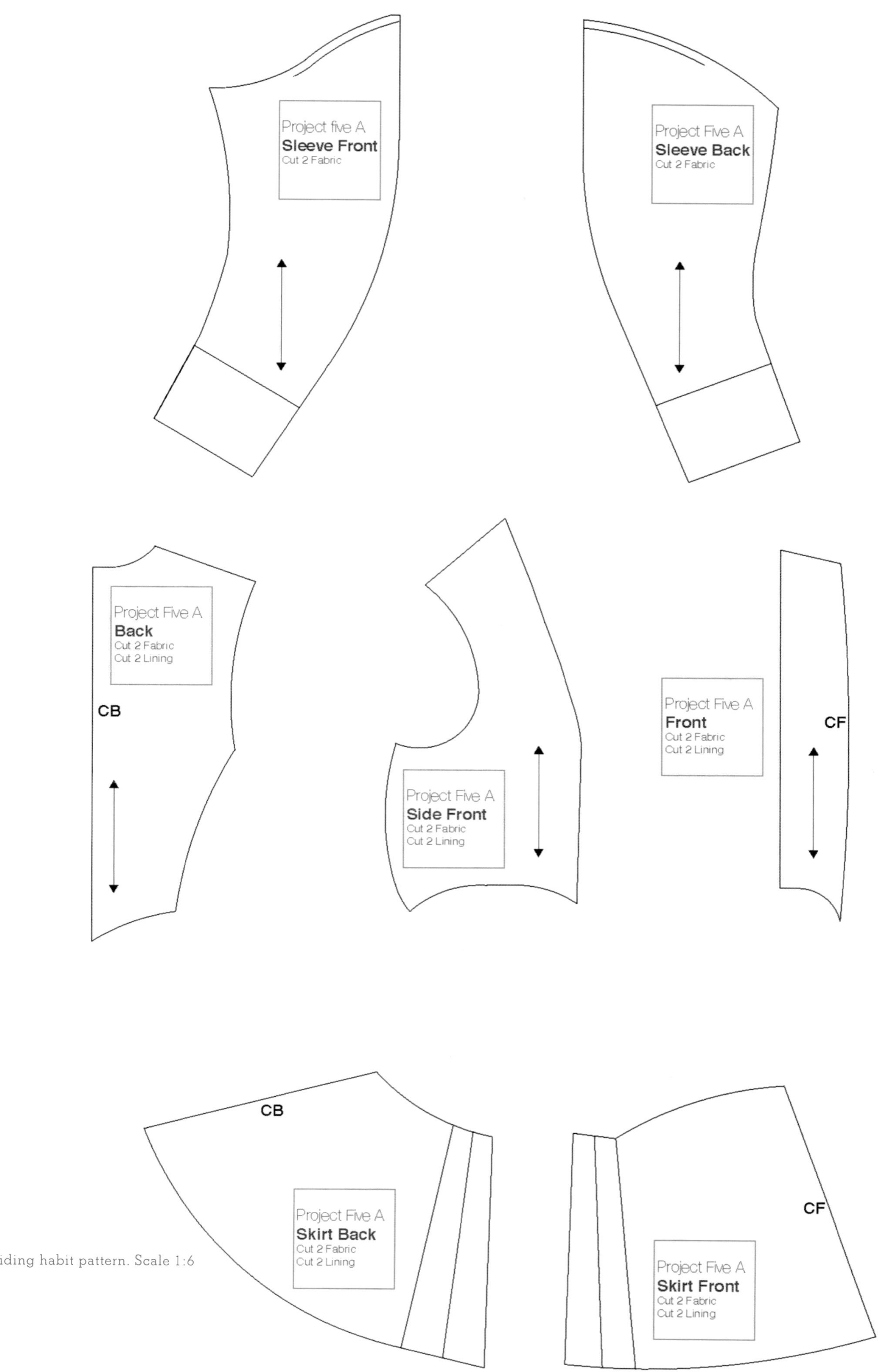

Riding habit pattern. Scale 1:6

Chapter 11 – Project 6: *Robe à la Polonaise*, 1780

Gulliver's Travels, Jonathan Swift[1]

Robe à la polonaise

Alison is wearing the now fashionable *robe à la polonaise*, which continued to be fashionable wear until the 1790s. Shorter in the skirts, with the overskirts hitched up to show off the underskirts, this was the perfect costume in which to go walking. Walking and admiring the fashions of others was a popular activity at this time in the period, as the novel *Evelina* by Frances Burney attests:

> The walk was very agreeable to us; everyone looked gay and seemed pleased; and the ladies were so much dressed, that Miss Mirvan and I could do nothing but look at them.[2]

As Alison's overskirt uses buttons to hitch it up, it could also be worn with the overskirt unbuttoned and not gathered. The underskirt is a quilted silk petticoat, which would have provided extra warmth. It was also a fashion statement, as normal, practical items became more fancy and on show.

Alison wears a shift, long stays with boning across the bust line, and pads under her costume. You can find the patterns for these in Chapter 16. Her stockings and shoes are now more important as they are seen.

She wears gloves and carries a parasol ready for an afternoon promenade. See Chapter 5 for more information on other suitable accessories.

What You Will Need

The following will give you an estimate of what you will need. However, as fabric widths vary and patterns may be resized, you should double-check how much fabric you need once you have drawn up your pattern.

Fabrics: Between 5 and 6 metres depending on the width of the fabric, but it is best to check once you have scaled up your pattern.

Petticoat/overskirt: You will need to cut between two and three panels for each, depending on the fabric width and your personal preference. See Chapter 16 for more information.

Other: Large hooks and eyes. Buttons and ribbon for loops.

The Bodice

The following instructions are for making the bodice with a lining but leaving the sleeves unlined. If you don't want to line the bodice, you will need to finish the raw edges of the seams and all other edges as you go along. If you wish to line the sleeves, you can use the same pattern and add sleeves to your bodice lining as described for the outer sleeves.

1. Stitch the bodice pieces together, starting from the centre back of the bodice and working outwards to the front. Press.

2. Next, stitch and press the shoulder seams. At this stage you are now ready for a fitting.

Make up the bodice lining in the same way.

The Sleeves

1. Stitch each sleeve together, then the raw edges and press.

2. Now fit the sleeves into the bodice. I like to have the sleeve with the right side facing, and fit it into the bodice with the bodice on the outside. However you do it, ensure you are putting the right sides of the sleeve and bodice together and double-check before stitching.

3. Start at the bottom (the underarm) and work up to the top. When you get to the section of the sleeve that is marked on the pattern, pin-tuck or gather the extra fullness into the sleeve hole, making sure both sides match.

4. When you are happy with the way your sleeve looks, stitch it onto the bodice. It is well worth taking the time to get this right.

Lining the Bodice

Lining the bodice will cover up all the raw edges. If you wish to line your bodice, it should be attached at this stage.

1. Pin the outer and lining pieces together with the right sides together and stitch around the edge, leaving a gap to allow you to turn it the right sid out.

2. Mitre the corners and trim down the seam allowances before turning the bodice the right side out. Gently push out the corners and curves before pressing.

3. Next, tuck the raw edges inward and stitch the lining over the gap and sleeve holes. Ideally, stitch this

The front of the gown.

The back of the gown.

The side of the gown.

by hand. If you prefer, you can use bias binding for the sleeve holes.

Finishing the Bodice

1. Finish the bodice by hemming the bottom edges of the sleeve and by stitching hooks and eyes down the front of the bodice. Alternating the sides on which you stitch the hooks and eyes will ensure the bodice stays closed.

2. At this point, you can also stitch a decorative trim to the neckline and cuffs if you wish.

The Overskirt

1. Stitch the panels together and finish the edges if needed.

2. Turn over the skirt side edges twice and stitch.

3. Turn up the hem twice and stitch.

4. Establish the button placement. Put the skirt on the stand to do this; it will help you see what looks best. Stitch on the buttons and sew ribbon loops onto the hem directly below the buttons or under the hem.

5. Gather or pleat the skirt until it fits the waist of the bodice, as marked on the pattern. Stitch the overskirt to the bodice.

The Quilted Petticoat

1. Stitch up the side seams on the fabric and lining.

2. Pin the fabric and lining with the right sides together and pin the wadding on the outside.

3. Stitch around the bottom, trim and turn. Top-stitch the hem 2.5cm up from the seam.

4. Complete quilting as shown in Chapter 3.

5. Finish the waistband by trimming away the wadding as needed. Then turn the fabric and lining inwards and top-stitch through it again 2.5cm further down.

6. Next make a gap in the inside of the lining seam, and overstitch at the top and bottom of the gap to ensure it doesn't come undone any further.

7. Attach a safety pin to your cord and feed the cord through the casing until it comes back out. Keep the cord tied to stop it coming out when the skirt is not worn.

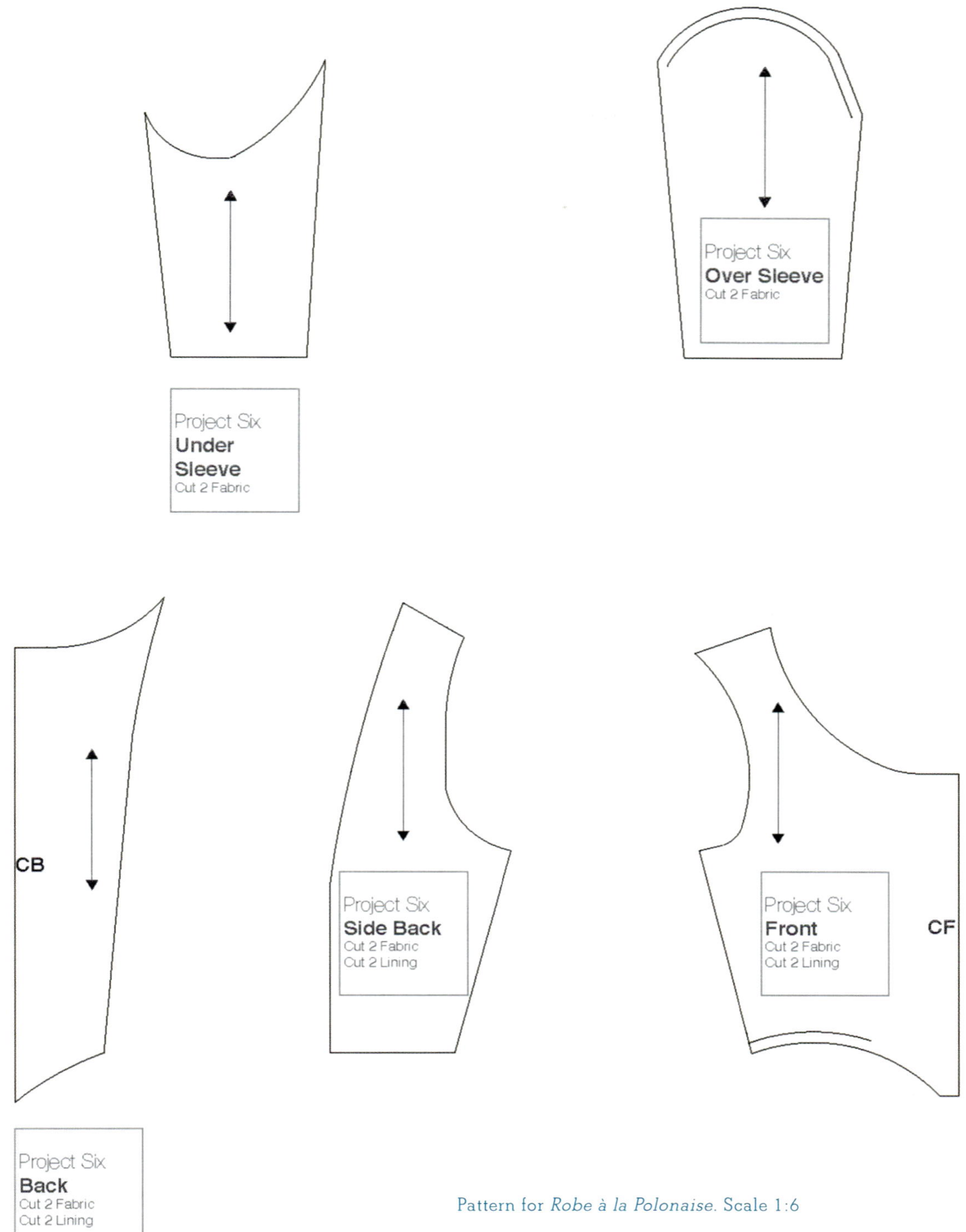

Pattern for *Robe à la Polonaise*. Scale 1:6

WAYS TO WEAR YOUR *ROBE À LA POLONAISE*

You can make your *robe à la polonaise* with more than two gathers and three puffs. Try experimenting with different amounts of skirt fullness and the number of gathers to create different looks.

Chapter 12 – Project 7: *Chemise à la reine, 1790*

Chemise à la reine

Kirsten wears a version of the *chemise à la reine,* popularized by Marie Antoinette as an escape from the formal fashions of court. This dress was the turning point for fashion in this period, and was made of cotton and fine Indian muslin printed with a sprig print. Such dresses needed no more than a coloured sash to complete them. It was first greeted with shock, but later merged into the new streamlined French look. Accessible to most women and simpler to wear, it leads the way for the Regency fashions to come.

As this dress keeps the formal structure, Kirsten still wears the standard shift and long stays with boning across the bust line, together with a standard petticoat and small pad as the skirt is still quite full. You can find the patterns for the shift, stays, pad and petticoat in Chapter 16.

Kirsten wears her dress with a sash, fichu and a straw hat. The pattern for the neckerchief can be found in Chapter 16. See Chapter 5 for more information on other suitable accessories.

What You Will Need

The following will give you an estimate of what you will need. However, as fabric widths vary and patterns may be resized, you should double-check how much fabric you need once you have drawn up your pattern.

Fabrics: Between 6 and 7 metres, for both the underneath and upper layers, depending on the width of the fabric, but it is best to check once you have scaled up your pattern.

Skirt: You will need to cut between two and three panels depending on the fabric width and your personal preference. See Chapter 16 for more information.

Other: Buttons, ribbon for lacing or lacing tape.

The Bodice

As this dress is already made up of two layers, I haven't lined it, but you could make up a lining if you wish.

1. Start by laying the sheer fabric pieces over the top of the cotton pieces and pleat the sheer layer until the two match. Even out the pleats across each piece using pins, much like pin tucks.

2. Once you are happy with the way the pleats look, turn the pieces over and use a running stitch to sew them, while trying not to let your stitching show on the right side, as you do with a slip stitch. Work you way along each piece with about 1.5cm spacing between each line of stiching.

3. When you have finished, steam each piece, but don't press them.

4. Stitch the bodice pieces together at the side and shoulder seams, leaving the centre back open. At this stage you are ready for a fitting.

The front of the gown.

The Sleeves

1. Stitch each sleeve together, leaving a gap at the cuff as marked on the pattern. Finish the raw seam edges and press.

2. Now fit the sleeves into the bodice. I like to have the sleeve with the right side facing, and fit it into the bodice with the bodice on the

The back of the gown.

The side of the gown.

Shown with a purple silk ribbon sash.

3. Stitch the skirts onto the bodice, then finish and hem both skirts.

The Sash

1. Put the right sides of the sash pieces together and stitch around the raw edges, leaving a gap to turn it the right side out.

2. Mitre the corners and trim down the seam allowances, then turn the sash the right side out. Gently push out the corners before pressing.

3. Finish by stitching up the gap.

outside. However you do it, ensure you are putting the right sides of the sleeve together and double-check before stitching.

3. Start at the bottom (the underarm) and work up to the top. When you get to the section of the sleeve that is marked on the pattern, pin-tuck or gather the extra fullness into the sleeve hole, making sure both sides match.

4. When you are happy with the way your sleeve looks, stitch the sleeve onto the bodice. It is well worth taking the time to get this right.

Back Lacing

1. Turn over the centre back bodice edges twice and finish.

2. Pin loops of ribbon, cord or whatever you plan to use for the front lacing down the centre back facing towards the centre back opening, with spacing to suit the size of the cord or ribbon that you plan to use as lacing. Make sure that when they are laced, there won't be a gap at the back. Make sure you stitch the loops on securely.

Finishing the Bodice

1. Stitch the buttons and ribbon loops to the opening at the cuff.

2. Turn under the neckline edge twice and stitch.

The Skirt

1. Stitch the panels of the outer skirt together and press. Repeat for the underskirt.

2. Tack the two skirts together at the top, then gather or pleat both until they are the same measurement as the bodice waist.

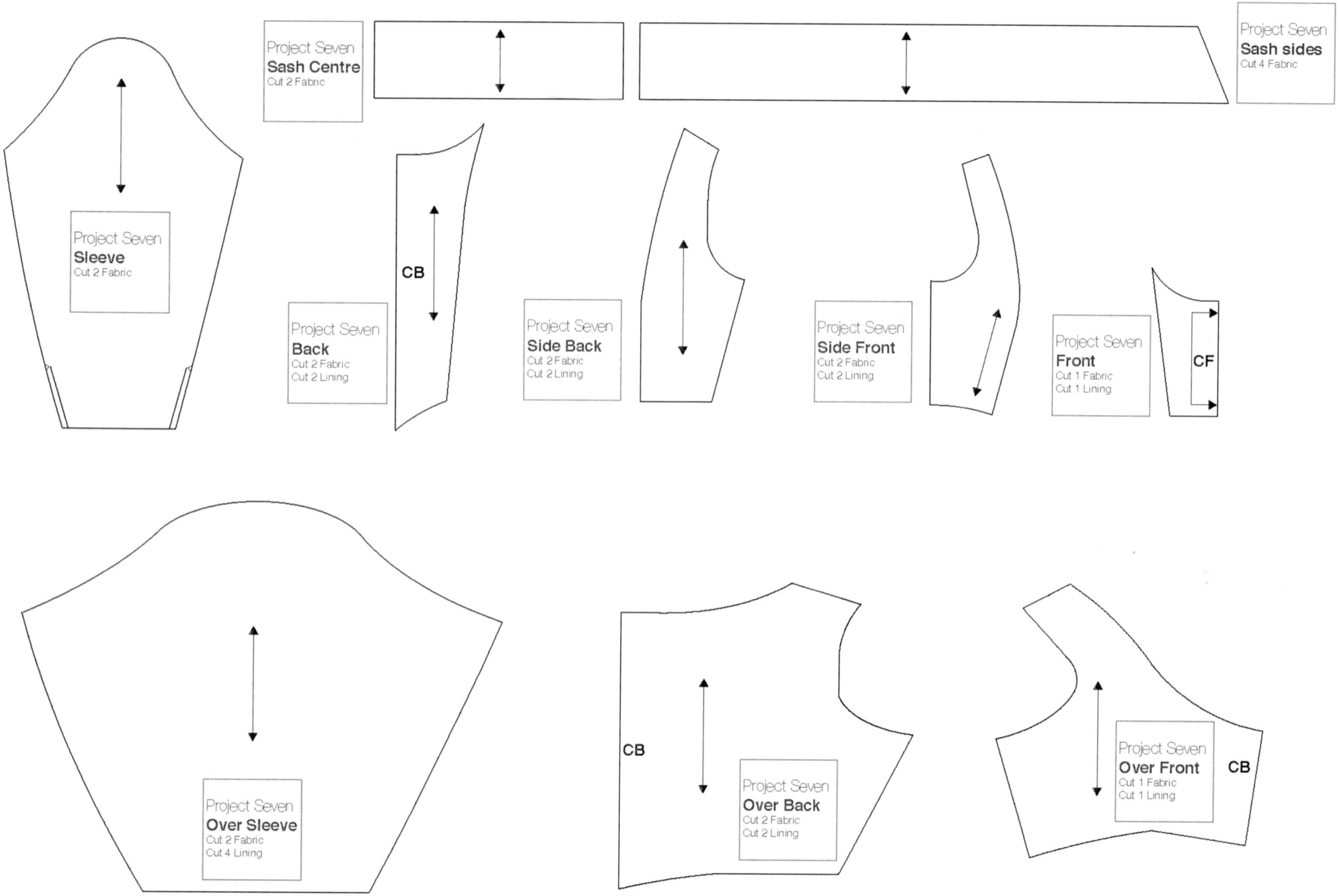

Pattern for *Chemise à la Reine*. Scale 1:8

Chapter 13 – Project 8: Directoire Gown and Circus Costume, 1800

Directoire Gown

Camille wears a dress made popular by
Joséphine Bonaparte, later Empress of
France. In this latest style, her dress is
simple and elegant, made from crisp
white muslin and lined with cotton.
Short puffed sleeves, long slim skirts and
a wide neckline mean a lot less fabric is
required.

Worn first in France and soon
spreading out across Europe and the
colonies, this was the beginning of a
new style that developed into what is
today commonly called the Regency
style. The Regency itself was later,
starting in 1811, by which time the
fashion was established. Although this
dress was cotton, it was considered
appropriate for evening and formal wear.

A lighter fashion meant lighter layers.
The shift was still worn, and most women
continued to wear stays; however, the
new high waistline meant that wearing
short stays and sometimes a small central
back pad were possible. You can find the
patterns for the shift, stays, pad and
petticoat in Chapter 16.

Accessories such as shawls allowed
women to keep warm in such light
fashions. Gloves were still worn and fans
were carried. See Chapter 5 for more
information on other suitable
accessories.

What You Will Need

The following will give you an estimate
of what you will need. However, as
fabric widths vary and patterns may be
resized, you should double-check how
much fabric you need once you have
drawn up your pattern.

Fabrics: Between 6 and 7 metres
depending on the width of the
fabric, but it is best to check once
you have scaled up your pattern.

Skirt: You will need to cut between
two and three panels depending on
the fabric width and your personal
preference. See Chapter 16 for
more information.

Other: Ribbon and binding for
ties.

The Bodice

The following instructions are for
making the bodice with a lining but
leaving the sleeves unlined. If you
don't want to line the bodice, you will
need to finish the raw edges of the
seams and all other edges at each
stage. If you wish to line the sleeves,
you can use the same pattern and add
sleeves to your bodice lining as
described for the outer sleeves.

1. Pleat the centre fronts of the
   bodice to suit, making sure both
   sides match.

2. Stitch the bodice together from
   centre front around to centre back,
   leaving the back open. Press.

3. Stitch the shoulders and press.

4. Gather or pleat under the bust as
   marked on the pattern. Pleats
   should face inwards towards the
   centre front. At this stage you are
   ready for a fitting.

   Make up the bodice lining in the
   same way.

The front of the gown.

The Sleeves

1. Stitch each sleeve together, then
   finish the raw edges and press.

2. Now fit the sleeve into the bodice.
   I like to have the sleeve with the
   right side facing, and fit it into the
   bodice with the bodice on the
   outside. However you do it, ensure
   you are putting the right sides of

The back of the gown.

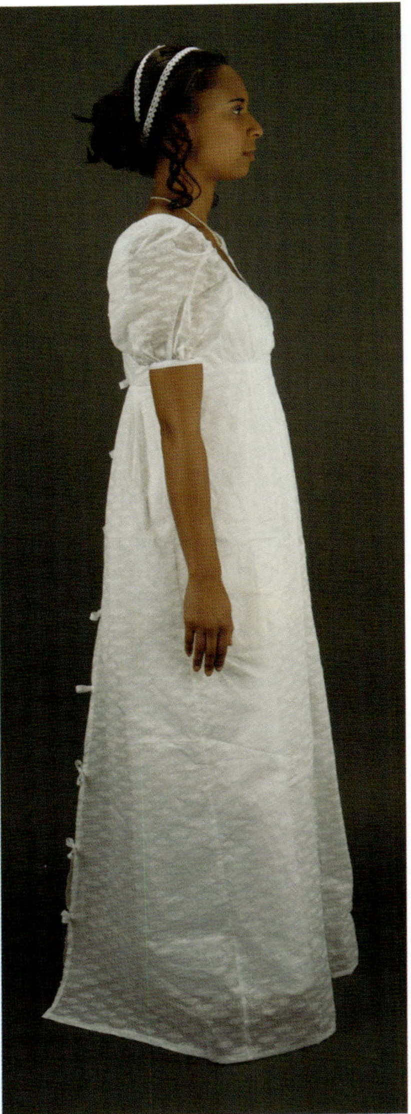

The side of the gown.

SHEER SEAMS

Original dresses made from sheer fabrics often had French seams. Ideally, these should be as narrow as you can make them.

2. Mitre the corners and trim down the seam allowances. Turn the bodice the right side out. Gently push out the corners and curves before pressing.

3. Next tuck the raw edges inward and stitch the lining over the gap and sleeve holes. Ideally, stitch this by hand. If you prefer, you can use bias binding for the sleeve holes.

5. Evenly space and stitch the bows down the centre back of the gown.

The Skirt

1. Stitch the overskirt together, leaving centre back open.

2. Next stitch the skirt lining together, leaving a gap at the centre back as marked on the pattern.

3. Turn under the centre back edges of the overskirt twice and stitch.

4. Starting at the centre back, make knife pleats until the skirt fits flat across the front of the bodice.

5. Stitch the skirt and skirt lining to the bodice.

Finishing

Evenly space and stitch the ties down the centre back of the gown.

---

the sleeve and bodice together and double-check before stitching.

3. Start at the bottom (the underarm) and work up to the top. When you get to the section of the sleeve that is marked on the pattern, pin-tuck or gather the extra fullness into the sleeve hole, making sure both sides match.

4. When you are happy with the way your sleeve looks, stitch it onto the bodice. It is well worth taking the time to get this right.

5. Next gather the cuffs to the size of

your upper arm and use bias binding to cover the raw edge of the cuff. Stitch over the top of the binding to finish.

Lining the Bodice

Lining the bodice will cover up all your raw edges. If you wish to line your bodice, it should be attached at this stage.

1. Pin the outer and lining pieces together with the right sides together and stitch around the edge, leaving a gap to allow you to turn it the right side out.

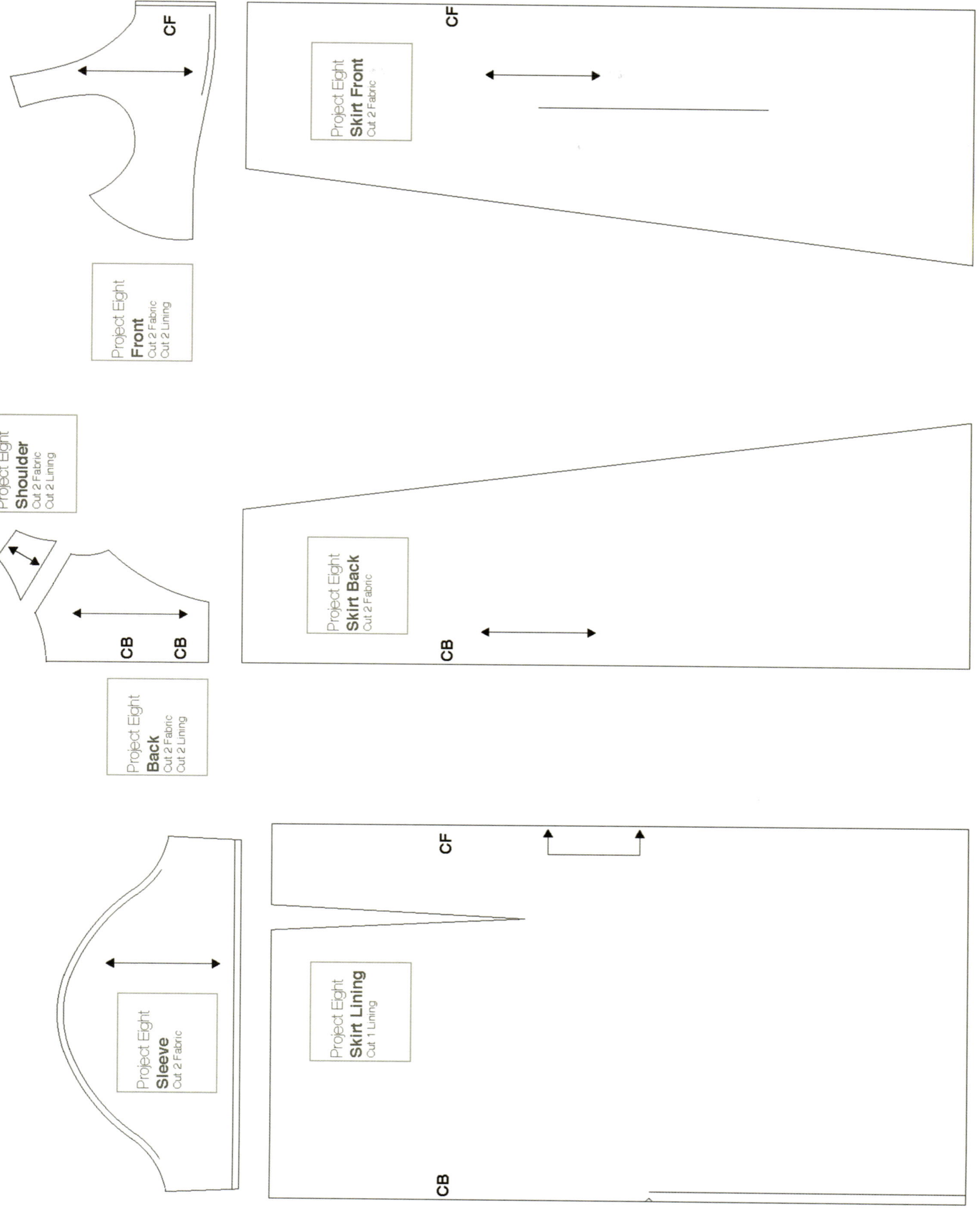

Early Directoire pattern. Scale 1:8

Directoire Gown as a Circus Costume

> I was diverted with none so much as
> that of the rope-dancers.
>
> *Gulliver's Travels,* Jonathan Swift[2]

Camille is a circus performer, a rope-walker. The changes in fashion allowed performers a new freedom of dress. Shorter dresses meant the audience could see the performers' legs, allowing more complex tricks to be completed, and to be better appreciated by the audience.

Most performers had to cover the costs of their own costumes, but these also needed to be eye-catching. The cost of such costumes meant they also needed to be hard-wearing, carefully kept and mended as needed. This dress could also work as a masquerade costume.

Camille wears a shift and short stays under her costume; you can find the patterns for these in Chapter 16.

The accessories are two interwoven sashes and golden wings. Wings such as these were worn by performers whose tricks seemed to defy gravity. A hoop or balance stick would also make suitable accessory for a rope-walker.

To make a circus costume, follow the early Directoire pattern for the bodice and cut your skirt by following the instructions in Chapter 16.

Camille practises her balancing act.

What You Will Need

The following will give you an estimate of what you will need. However, as fabric widths vary and patterns may be resized, you should double-check how much fabric you need once you have drawn up your pattern.

Fabrics: Between 4 and 5 metres depending on the width of the fabric, but it is best to check once you have scaled up your pattern.

Skirt: You will need to cut between two and three panels depending on the fabric width and your personal preference. See Chapter 16 for more information.

Other: Sinamay (millinery fabric), gold spray paint for the wings, lacing, binding for the edges.

The Bodice

Use the bodice pattern for the Directoire gown. The following instructions are for making the bodice with a lining but leaving the sleeves unlined. If you don't want to line the bodice, you will need to finish the raw edges of the seams and all other edges at each stage. If you wish to line the sleeves, you can use the same pattern and add sleeves to your bodice lining as described for the outer sleeves.

1. Stitch the bodice together from centre front around to centre back, leaving the back open. Press.

2. Next stitch the shoulder seams and press.

3. Gather or pleat under the bust as marked on the pattern. Pleats should face inwards towards the centre front. At this stage you are ready for a fitting.

Make the bodice lining in the same way.

The Sleeves

1. Stitch each sleeve together, then finish the raw edges and press.

2. Now fit the sleeves into the bodice. I like to have the sleeve with the right side facing, and fit it into the bodice with the bodice on the outside. However you do it, ensure you are putting the right sides of the sleeve and bodice together and double check before stitching.

3. Start at the bottom (the underarm) and work up to the top. When you get to the section of the sleeve that is marked on the pattern, pin-tuck or gather the extra fullness into the sleeve hole, making sure both sides match.

4. When you are happy with the way your sleeve looks, stitch the sleeve onto the bodice. It is well worth taking the time to get this right.

5. Next gather the cuffs to the size of your upper arm and use bias binding to cover the raw edge of the cuff. Stitch over the top of the binding to finish.

The Bodice Lining

Lining in to the bodice will cover up all the raw edges. If you wish to line your bodice, it should be attached at this stage.

1. Pin the outer and lining pieces together with the right sides together and stitch around the edge, leaving a gap to allow you to turn it the right side out.

2. Mitre the corners and trim down the seam allowances before turning the bodice the right side out. Gently push out the corners and curves before pressing.

3. Next tuck the raw edges inward and stitch the lining over the gap and sleeve holes. Ideally, stitch this by hand. If you prefer, you can use bias

The front of the gown.

The back of the gown.

The side of the gown.

The side of the gown with sash and wings.

binding for the sleeve holes.

The Skirt

1. Start by stitching the panels together and finishing any raw edges.

2. Gather the top of the skirt to fit the waistband, making sure you even out the fullness. It should be nearly flat at the front and full at the back. Tack and stitch the skirt to the waistband when you are happy.

3. Determine the correct length of the skirt, then turn up the bottom edge of the skirt twice and stitch.

Finishing

Evenly space and stitch the ties down the centre back of the gown.

The back of the gown with sash and wings.

The Wings

Camille's wings have been cut from sinamay (millinery fabric), pressed into shape, spray-painted gold and pinned to the centre back of her gown.

The Sashes

Camille's sashes are made from a length of tulle and a length of ribbon twisted together and tied round the waist.

WAYS TO WEAR YOUR CIRCUS COSTUME

This dress is based on an original French watercolour of a female rope-walker at this time. The only difference between the dress shown here and the original image is that the original dress appears to have large gold stars on it. If you want to create the dress with the stars, you could look out for a white or cream silk with a star print.

Chapter 14 – Project 9: Regency Gown and Spencer, 1815

Regency Gown

Bryony wears the classic Regency look, the style we associate with Jane Austen and her novels. Bryony's dress could be day wear or evening wear depending on how it is made up. Long sleeves are normally considered to be day wear, but the fine sheer silk this dress is made up in is more suitable for a formal occasion. Made up in cotton, it could be worn as a walking costume.

This is a front-fastening bib-front gown. The underfronts lace at the centre front, with splits in the dress ether side down the skirts. The bib front of the bodice is stitched to the skirt front and flaps up over the lacing, buttoning to the bodice at the corners of the bib front and the skirt flaps. It is easy to put on and to wear.

Under her sheer silk dress, Bryony wears one of the coloured petticoats that so amused Jane Austen. Her petticoat is cut in the new slim style. She also wears a shift and short stays – pads are no longer worn. You can find the patterns for the shift, stays and petticoat in Chapter 16.

Now that skirts are so slim, pockets have been replaced by reticules. For day wear a bonnet in the new shape, called a poke bonnet, would have been worn. You can find a pattern for the reticule in Chapter 16. See Chapter 5 for more information on other suitable accessories.

What You Will Need

The following will give you an estimate of what you will need. However, as fabric widths vary and patterns may be resized, you should double-check how much fabric you need once you have drawn up your pattern.

Fabrics: Between 6 and 7 metres, for both the underneath and top layers, depending on the width of the fabric, but it is best to check once you have scaled up your pattern.

Skirt: You will need to cut between two and three panels depending on the fabric width and your personal preference. See Chapter 16 for more information.

Other: Buttons, ribbon for the button loops, a large hook and eye for the Spencer, ribbon for lacing or lacing tape for the dress centre front.

The Gown

The following instructions are for making the bodice and train with a lining but leaving the sleeves unlined. If you don't want to line the bodice or train, you will need to finish the raw edges of the seams and all other edges at each stage. If you wish to line the sleeves, you can use the same pattern and add sleeves to your bodice lining as described for the outer sleeves. However, this dress – in fine silk – has been made up unlined.

1. Stitch the bodice together from the centre back round to the front, which should be left open. Finish and press the seams.

2. Stitch the shoulder seams, finish and press.

3. For an unlined bodice, finish the top and side edges of the flap front. If you are adding a lining, pin the outer and lining pieces together with the right sides together and stitch them together, leaving the bottom open. Mitre the corners and trim down the seam allowances. Then turn the panel

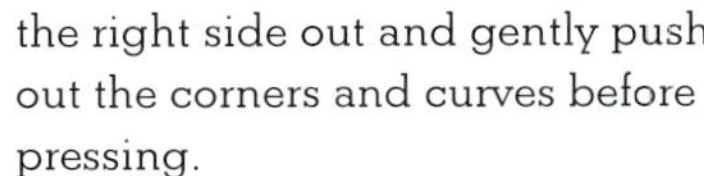

The back of the gown.

The side of the gown.

The front of the Spencer.

the right side out and gently push out the corners and curves before pressing.

4. Finally, gather under the bust as marked on the pattern. At this stage you are ready for a fitting.

If you are lining the bodice, make up the lining in the same way.

The Sleeves

1. Stitch each sleeve together, finish the raw edges and press.

2. Now fit the sleeve into the bodice. I like to have the sleeve with the right side facing, and fit it into the bodice with the bodice on the

outside. However you do it, ensure you are putting the right sides of the sleeve and bodice together and double-check before stitching.

3. Start at the bottom (the underarm) and work up to the top. When you get to the section of the sleeve that is marked on the pattern, pin-tuck or gather the extra fullness into the sleeve hole, making sure both sides match.

4. When you are happy with the way your sleeve looks, stitch the sleeve onto the bodice. It is well worth taking the time to get this right.

The Skirt

1. Stitch the skirt panels together.

2. Then hand-finish the slits in the front by turning the edges over twice and overstitching the point, in a similar fashion to a gore but without the insert (see Chapter 3).

3. Following the pattern markings, pleat or gather the back and sides of the skirt until they fit the relevant bodice pieces.

4. Next stitch the bib front to the central skirt panel, matching centre front to centre front.

5. Finally, stitch the main bodice to the back of the skirt matching centre back to centre back.

6. For an unlined bodice, turn over the neckline edge twice and stitch.

The back of the Spencer.

The side of the Spencer.

The Bodice Lining

Lining the bodice will cover up all the raw edges. If you wish to line your bodice, it should be attached at this stage.

1. Pin the outer bodice and lining pieces together with the right sides together and stitch around the edge, leaving a gap to allow you to turn it the right side out.

2. Mitre the corners and trim down the seam allowances before turning the bodice the right side out. Gently push out the corners and curves before pressing.

3. Next tuck the raw edges inward and stitch the lining over the gap and sleeve holes. Ideally, stitch this

by hand. If you prefer, you can use bias binding for the sleeve holes.

Front Lacing

1. Hand-stitch eyelets down both sides of the centre front of both bodice panels as marked on the pattern.

2. You will need to establish where the buttons to hold your bib front up should be stitched while you are wearing it. Stitch ribbon loops on both of the top corners of your bib front.

Finishing

Hem the cuffs and skirts to complete your gown.

The Spencer jacket

The Spencer jacket, named after Earl Spencer, was needed to protect women from the cold in these new slimline fashions. It is a classic Regency style and was first worn as far back as 1790, and continued to be worn until 1820 when waistlines started to drop. Its practicality might be part of the reason it was so popular and widely worn.

Jacket Body

1. Stitch the jacket body together from the centre back round to the front, which should be left open. Finish and press the seams.

2. Stitch the shoulder seams, finish and press. At this stage you are ready for a fitting.

Make up the Spencer lining in the same way.

The Collar

1. Stitch the collar seams together and press.

2. Then apply interfacing to one side of the collar, using either iron-on or sew-in interfacing.

3. Pin the right sides of the two collar pieces together, then stitch around the sides and top, leaving a gap where the collar joins the jacket.

4. Mitre the corners and trim down the seam allowances before turning the collar the right side out. Gently push out the corners and curves before pressing.

5. Stitch the underside of the collar to the jacket neck, matching centre back seams. Press the raw edge under and hand-stitch down.

6. Make up the Spencer tails by stitching around the sides and ends. Mitre the corners and trim down the seam allowances.

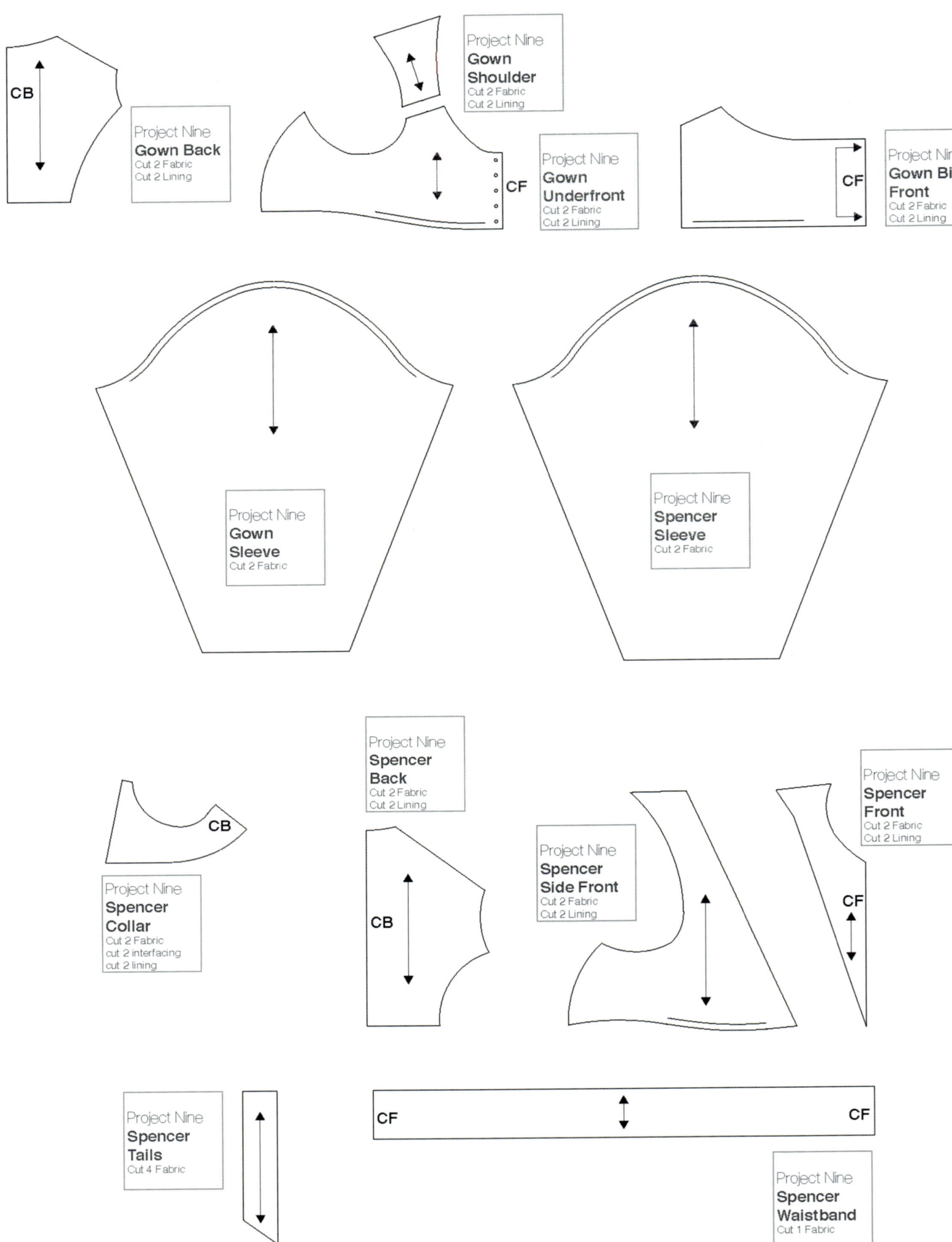

Pattern for Regency Gown and Spencer. Scale 1:8

A length of ribbon is a simple way
to dress up and add colour to a
costume.

7. Pin your tails on the centre back of
the bodice facing up towards the
neck, right side to right side. At
this stage you are ready for a
fitting.

Jacket Waistband

1. Place interfacing over the
waistband, fold in half and stitch
at each end.

2. Mitre the corners and trim down
the seam allowances. Then turn the
waistband the right side out and
gently push out the corners and
curves before pressing.

3. Pleat or gather the jacket bodice as
marked on the pattern, until it fits
the waistband, making sure both
sides are even and the pleats are
evenly spaced. The centre back of
the waistband should match the
centre back of the jacket.

4. Stitch the outside of the waistband
to the bodice, stitching the tails in
at the same time. Then press under
the raw edge of the open side
ready to catch it in the lining.

The Sleeves

1. Stitch each sleeve together, then
finish the raw edges and press.

2. Now fit the sleeves into the jacket. I
like to have the sleeve with the
right side facing, and fit it into the
bodice with the jacket on the
outside. However you do it, ensure
you are putting the right sides of
the sleeve and jacket together and
double-check before stitching.

3. Start at the bottom (the underarm)
and work up to the top. When you
get to the section of the sleeve that
is marked on the pattern, pin-tuck
or gather the extra fullness into the
sleeve hole, making sure both sides
match.

4. When you are happy with the way
your sleeve looks, stitch the sleeve
onto the bodice. It is well worth
taking the time to get this right.

ALTERNATIVE
AUSTEN

This pattern is the perfect starting
point for alternative Austen fans to
make a Comic Con costume based
on the parody mash-up novels
Pride and Prejudice and Zombies
or *Sense and Sensibility and Sea
Monsters*. Both books are full of
wonderful details that could be
worked into costumes.

QUICK CHANGES

If you need to change out of your
dress quickly, you could use
poppers on your bib front opening
rather then loops, buttons and
lacing. Stitch poppers on the
underside of the fabric so they
cannot be seen when you are
wearing it and stitch buttons over
the top to disguise the modern
fastening.

The Jacket Lining

Lining the jacket will cover up all the
raw edges. If you wish to line your
jacket, it should be attached at this
stage.

1. Pin the outer and lining pieces
together with the right sides
together and stitch around the
edge, leaving a gap along the
waistband to allow you to turn it
the right side out.

2. Mitre the corners and trim down
the seam allowances. Turn the
jacket the right side out. Gently
push out the corners and curves
before pressing.

3. Next tuck the raw edges inward
and stitch the lining over the gap
and sleeve holes. Ideally, stitch this
by hand. At the waistband, tuck
the lining inside it and stitch as
before. If you prefer, you can use
bias binding for the sleeve holes.

4. Finish by turning over the raw
edges of the sleeve hems twice and
sewing.

Chapter 15 – Project 10: Late Regency Gown and Ballet Costume, 1825

Remember if you go to any dances next winter you will want a gown low to the neck.

Fanny Brawne to Fanny Keats[1]

Late Regency Gown

Georgia wears a late Regency style dress, perfect for attending a dance. Fashions have now started to change and the shape is starting to look Victorian. Waistlines are dropping, sleeves are getting larger and skirts are getting fuller.

Georgia wears a shift and short stays under her dress. By this stage many women would have been wearing drawers and the new longer stays with the central bust. To keep the fuller shape, wider petticoats were worn, sometimes more than one, and sometimes corded to better keep the shape – the layers are starting to build up again. Should you wish to, you could even wear sleeve pads with this dress to better hold the shape of your sleeves. You can find the patterns for the shift, stays and petticoat in Chapter 16.

Small items would be carried in a reticule and gloves would have been worn for formal events. Bonnets were also changing, opening up to show more of the face, and were worn outside with a Spencer or a cape for warmth. See Chapter 5 for more information on other suitable accessories.

What You Will Need

The following will give you an estimate of what you will need. However, as fabric widths vary and patterns may be resized, you should double-check how much fabric you need once you have drawn up your pattern.

Fabrics: Between 4 and 7 metres depending on the width of the fabric, but it is best to check once you have scaled up your pattern.

Skirt: You will need to cut between two and three panels depending on the fabric width and your personal preference. See Chapter 16 for more information.

Other: Ribbon for lacing or lacing tape.

The Bodice

The following instructions are for making the bodice with a lining but leaving the sleeves unlined. If you don't want to line the bodice, you will need to finish the raw edges of the seams and all other edges at each stage. If you wish to line the sleeves, you can use the same pattern and add sleeves to your bodice lining as described for the outer sleeves.

1. Stitch your bodice together working from the centre front round to the centre back, which is left open.

2. Next stitch the shoulder seams together and press.

3. Stitch the bodice to the waistband. Your bodice should now be complete and open at the centre front. At this stage you are ready for a fitting

Make up the bodice lining in the same way.

The Sleeves

1. Stitch each sleeve together, finish the raw edges and press.

The front of the gown.

2. Now fit the sleeves into the bodice. I like to have the sleeve the right side facing and fit it into the bodice, with the bodice on the outside. However you do it, ensure you are putting the right sides of the sleeve and bodice together and double-check before stitching.

Left: Georgia is seated with a book.

Lining the Bodice

Lining in to the bodice will cover up all the raw edges. If you wish to line your bodice, it should be attached at this stage.

1. Pin the outer and lining pieces together with the right sides together and stitch around the edge, leaving a gap to allow you to turn it the right side out.

2. Mitre the corners and trim down the seam allowances. Turn the bodice the right side out. Gently push out the corners and curves before pressing.

3. Next tuck the raw edges inward and stitch the lining over the gap and sleeve holes. Ideally, stitch this by hand. If you prefer, you can use bias binding for the sleeve holes.

The Skirt

1. Start by stitching the panels together and finishing any raw edges.

2. Gather the top of the skirt to fit the waistband, making sure you even out the fullness. When you are happy with the way the gathers look, tack and stitch the skirt to the waistband.

3. Determine the correct length of the skirt, then turn up the bottom edge of the skirt twice and stitch.

WAYS TO WEAR YOUR LATE REGENCY GOWN

If you want to wear sleeve pads with your dress, you can use bust pads as sleeve pads. Either run a length of ribbon across the length of the wadding before rolling it up and tie this around the top of your arm, or tack the pad into the armhole. Make sure you tack it to the armhole and not to the top of the sleeve or it will have the opposite effect than is intended.

The back of the gown.

The side of the gown.

3. Matching the notches, start at the bottom (the underarm) and work up to the top. When you get to the section of the sleeve which is marked on the pattern, pin-tuck or gather the extra fullness into the sleeve hole, making sure both sides match.

4. When you are ready, stitch the sleeve onto the bodice. It is well worth taking the time to get this right.

5. Next, stitch the cuff bands together at the seam, ensuring they are the right size for your upper arm. Gather the bottom of the sleeve to fit the cuff band. Then stitch on the outside, and turn the cuff under to the inside, tucking the raw edge

inside before pressing and ensuring the stitching is closed.

Bodice Lacing

1. Turn the centre back bodice edges over twice and stitch.

2. Pin loops of ribbon, cord or whatever you plan to use for the front lacing down the centre back facing towards the side seams, with spacing to suit the size of the cord or ribbon that you plan to use as lacing. Make sure when they are laced there wont be a gap at the back. These loops will be stitched in with the lining, but you should also overstitch them now to reinforce them.

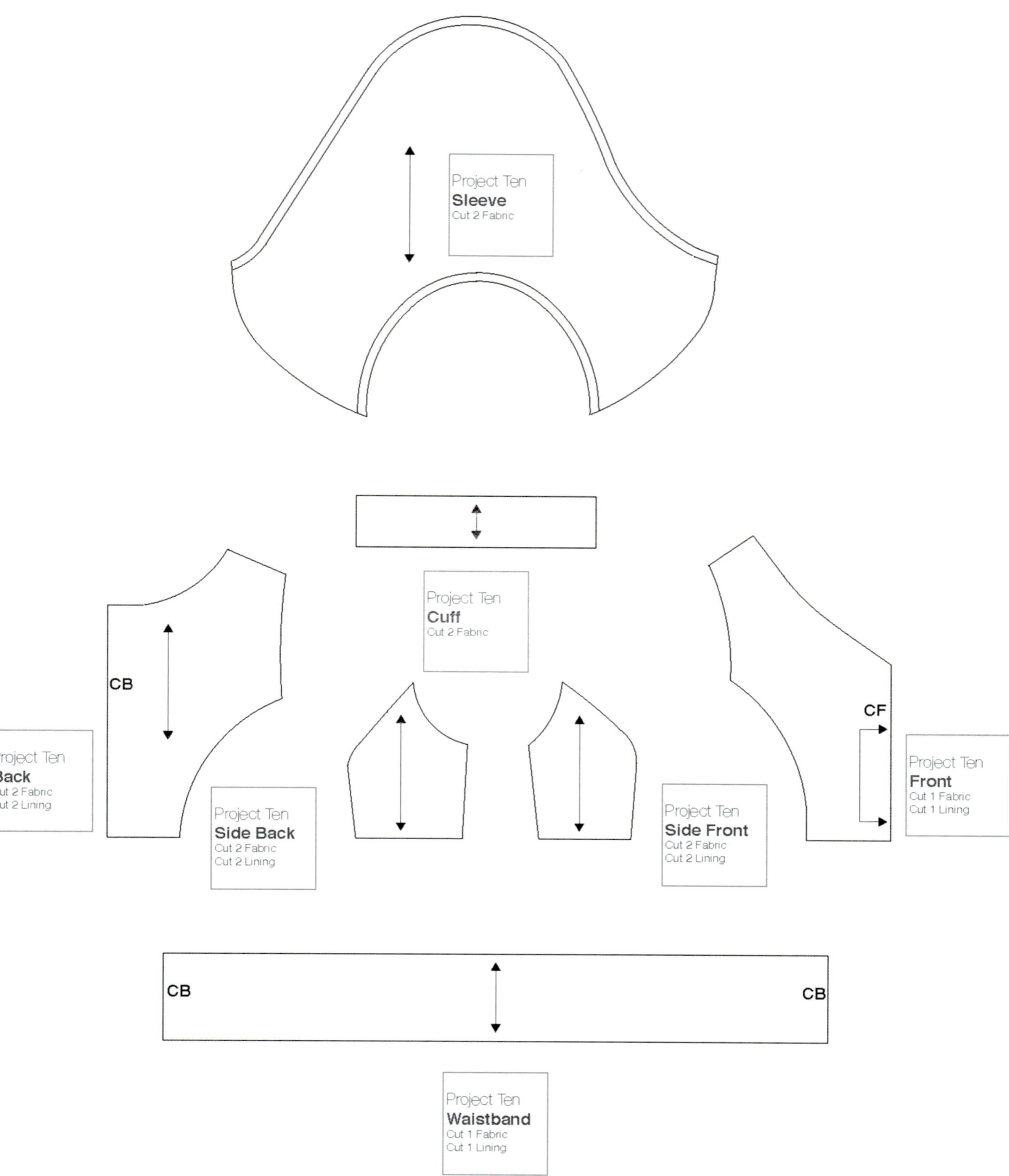

Pattern for Late Regency Gown. Scale 1:8

Georgia prepares to perform.

Late Regency Gown as an Early Romantic Ballet Costume

The human body is a machine which winds its own springs. It is the living image of perpetual movement.

L'homme machine, Julien Offray de La Mettrie[2]

Georgia wears an early Romantic ballet costume, one of the first versions of the tutu. The skirt of the dress is made from many layers of fine silk tulle. A costume like this in such bright shades would have stood out on the gas-lit stages of Regency theatre. Like other performers, ballet dancers benefitted from the fashion freedoms the new century brought. These were softer, lighter, shorter costumes that allowed dancers to move more freely and ensured the theatre seats were always full. This was a period in which ballet made great progress and started to become the art form we recognize today.

Ballet dancers were often responsible for the purchase and upkeep of their own costumes, which was a big ask on small salaries. A silk dress such as this would need to be worn many times to pay for itself. Georgia wears modern *pointe* shoes. The period equivalent would have been much softer and it would have been harder to stand *en pointe*, a skill which was already being performed and one which would be further developed by the advance of more supportive footwear.

Under her costume Georgia wears a shift and short stays. You can find the patterns for the shift and stays in Chapter 16.

Although not always suitable when dancing, accessories would have been used as props on stage if needed. See Chapter 5 for more information on other suitable accessories.

What You Will Need

Fabrics: Bodice, sleeves and sash: Between 2 and 3 metres.

Skirt: Fabric requirements for the tulle skirt can vary: we have used 8 metres in ours, but you may need more or less depending on how full you want it to be, what you can afford and the width of the fabric. It is best to check once you have scaled up your pattern.

Other: Ribbon for lacing or lacing tape.

The Bodice

The following instructions are for making the bodice and skirt with a lining but leaving the sleeves unlined. If you don't want to line the bodice, you will need to finish the raw edges of the seams and all other edges at each stage. If you wish to line the sleeves, you can use the same pattern and add sleeves to your bodice lining as described for the outer sleeves.

Use the bodice pattern from Project 10.

1. Stitch your bodice together. Work from the centre front around to the centre back, which is left open.

2. Next, stitch the shoulder seams together and press.

3. Stitch the bodice to the waistband. Your bodice should now be complete, and open at the centre back. At this stage you are ready for a fitting.

Make up the bodice lining in the same way.

Back Lacing

1. Turn over the centre back bodice edges twice and stitch.

2. Pin loops of ribbon, cord or whatever you plan to use for the back lacing down the centre backs facing towards the side seams, with spacing to suit the size of the cord or ribbon that you plan to use as lacing. Make sure that when they are laced there won't be a gap at the back. These loops will be stitched in with the lining, but

you should also overstitch them now to reinforce them.

Lining the Bodice

Lining the bodice will cover up all the raw edges. If you wish to line your bodice, it should be attached at this stage.

1. Pin the outer and lining pieces together with the right sides together and stitch around the edge, leaving a gap where the train is. This will allow you to turn it the right side out.

2. Mitre the corners and trim down the seam allowances. Turn the bodice the right side out. Gently push out the corners and curves before pressing.

3. Next tuck the raw edges inward

and stitch the lining over the gap and sleeve holes. Ideally, stitch this by hand. If you prefer, you can use bias binding for the sleeve holes.

The Sleeves

1. Stitch each sleeve together, then finish the raw edges and press.

2. Now fit the sleeves into the bodice. I like to have the sleeve with the right side facing, and fit it into the bodice with the bodice on the outside. However you do it, ensure you are putting the right sides of the sleeve and bodice together and double-check before stitching.

3. Start at the bottom (the underarm) and work up to the top. When you get to the section of the sleeve that is marked on the pattern, pin-tuck

The dress in motion.

or gather the extra fullness into the sleeve hole, making sure both sides match.

4. When you are happy with the way your sleeve looks, stitch it to the bodice. It is well worth taking the time to get this right.

5. Next stitch the cuff bands together at the seam, ensuring they are the right size for your upper arm. Gather the bottom of the sleeve to fit the cuff band. Stitch on the outside then turn the cuff under to the inside, tucking the raw edge inside before pressing and stitching closed.

The Skirt

1. Pre-cut your tulle to the desired length. The cut edge becomes the top of your skirt and the uncut edge is your finished hem edge. If you are unhappy with how the hem looks, you can bind it or turn it inside and stitch. However, it is best to do this at this stage due to the amount of fabric used.

2. For the lining, start by stitching the panels together and then finish any raw edges. Turn up the hem twice, making sure the lining is shorter then the tulle outer shirt, and stitch.

3. Pin the tulle and lining together, making sure you even out the fullness at the waist. When you are happy with the way this looks, tack and stitch the skirt to the waistband.

The Sash

Use the pattern from Project 7.

1. Put the right sides of the sash pieces together and stitch around the raw edges, leaving a gap to turn it the right side out.

2. Mitre the corners and trim down the seam allowances. Then turn the sash the right side out. Gently push out the corners before pressing.

3. Finish by stitching up the gap.

RED SHOES

Should you wish to match your satin ballet shoes to your dress, you can dye them. Georgia's are dyed with natural beetroot colouring and painted on with a brush, rather than dip-dyed, which gives an even colour while protecting the structure of the shoe.

Chapter 16 – Patterns for Underpinnings, Skirts, Petticoats and Accessories

Many young ladies make every thing they wear; by which means they can make a genteel figure at a small expense.

Hester Chapone[1]

Here are patterns for underpinnings and accessories that will give your costume an authentic look. Fabric requirements are given for each project. However, fabric widths vary, and patterns may be resized, you should double-check once you have drawn up your pattern.

Shift

This pattern has options for sleeves being short and elbow-length.

What you will need

Fabrics: Between 2 and 3 metres depending on the width of the fabric, but it is best to check once you have scaled up your pattern.

Other: Bias binding and cord for the neckline.

Instructions

1. If you are using a narrow fabric and the front and back pattern pieces are wider than your cloth, you will need to panel the sides of the shift together first. Finish the raw edges and press.

2. Stitch the shoulder seams together, finish and press.

3. For the shift with elbow-length sleeves, stitch bias binding as marked on the pattern. Attach the

Alison wears a shift with elbow-length sleeves.

cord to a safety pin and run it through the binding. Gather to fit just above the elbow and stitch the cord in place at each end.

4. Now, stitch the sleeves to the shift. Start by matching the centre of the sleeve cap to the shoulder seam, adding two or three pleats ether side and keeping them even both sides. When you are happy with how the sleeve looks, stitch it to the

body of the shift and finish the raw edge.

5. For a non-gusseted shift, place the rights sides of the shift front and back together, matching the underarm seams, then work outwards matching from the cuffs to the hem. Stitch, then clip into the armpit, stopping just before the seam. Finish and press.

6. For a gusseted shift, match the corners of the gusset square to the corners of the front and back seams. Then, working outwards, match from the cuffs to the hem. Stitch the sleeve and body of the shift up to the gusset by machine. It is best to stitch the gusset in by hand. Finish and press when complete.

7. Determine the correct length of the shift, then turn up the bottom edge twice and stitch. Hem the bottom of the sleeves.

8. Pin bias binding around the neckline edge. Stitch this down before turning the binding to the inside and pressing, tucking the raw edges in. Stitch the binding flat to the inside of the shift. Attach a cord to a safety pin and run this through the binding. Gather to fit and tie the cord.

SHIFT SUGGESTION

The cream three-quarter-sleeved shift has a broderie anglaise detail at the cuffs and hem. The cream linen had this detail along the selvage edge and the pattern was laid onto the fabric so that the detail could be used as part of the design.

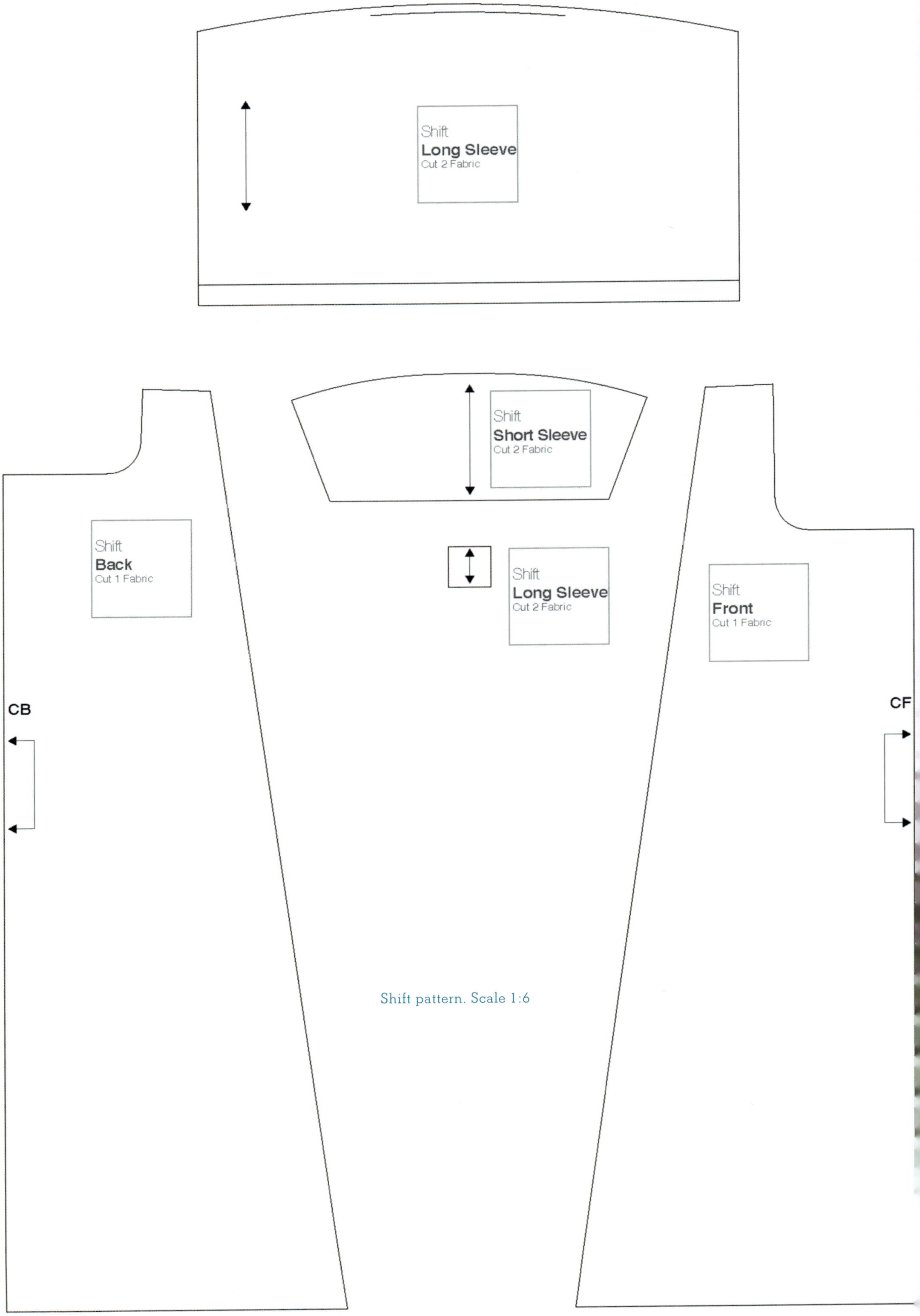

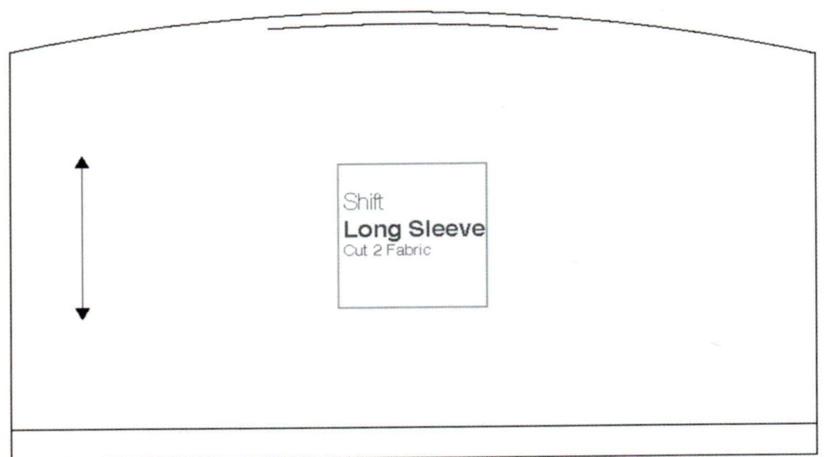

Shift
Long Sleeve
Cut 2 Fabric

Shift
Short Sleeve
Cut 2 Fabric

Shift
Long Sleeve
Cut 2 Fabric

Shift
Back
Cut 1 Fabric

Shift
Front
Cut 1 Fabric

CB

CF

Shift pattern. Scale 1:6

Kirsten wears a short-sleeved shift.

Long Stays

This pattern has options for different boning styles used during the earlier and later parts of our timeline. For earlier stays, follow only the vertical boning channels; for later stays, add the horizontal boning along the bust line. Later stays should be made up without the front lacing. This corset can also be made with or without a centre front opening.

What You Will Need

Fabrics: Between 0.5 and 1 metre both for the outer fabric and for the linen lining.

Other: Bias binding, cord, boning. We have used folded plastic boning to mimic the original bones, which would have been whalebone.

Instructions

I find it best to start by laying out all the pieces of fabric and lining in order.

1. Starting from the centre front and working outwards, pin and then stitch all the pieces together. This applies to both the outer layer and lining layer.

2. If you are making the stays with openings, stitch the centre front, leaving a gap as marked. If you want to have the centre front fully open, leave it open at this stage and finish it as you do for the back.

3. All but the centre front seams should be finished as felled seams, leaving room for boning in the seams. Fell the seams towards the centre back of the stays.

4. Place the outer fabric and lining layers together, making sure you have the right sides together before

Alison wears long stays.

The back of the long stays.

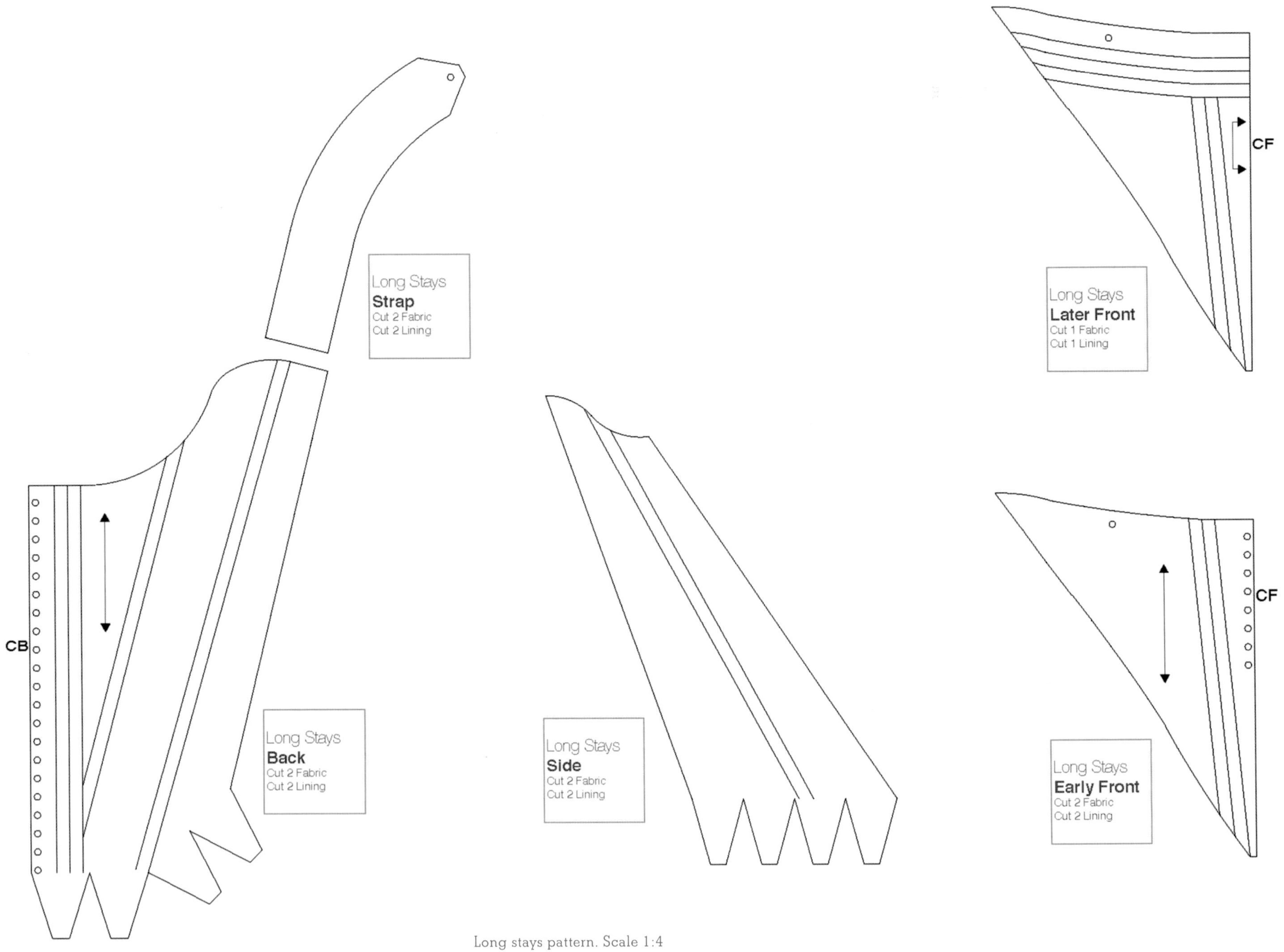

Long stays pattern. Scale 1:4

stitching down the centre back. If you are making stays with an open centre front, do the same to the centre front, then turn the right side out and press. However, if you are working with leather, do not press.

5. Stitch the boning channels as marked on the pattern; slide the boning between the channels, including those in between the seams. For the channels that end before the tabs at the waist, you need to hand-stitch the bottom edge to keep the boning in place.

6. If you are only having an opening at the top of the centre front of the stays, turn the raw edges of this opening inwards and hand-finish.

7. Next hand-stitch the eyelets as marked on the pattern.

8. Finally, apply bias binding to the raw edges at the top and bottom of your stays. I find it best to tack first with a running stitch before overstitching the binding.

Short Stays

This pattern has a centre back and front opening, but you can cut it with only front or back lacing if your prefer.

What You Will Need

Fabrics: About 0.5 metre both for the outer fabric and for the lining.

Other: Bias binding, cord, boning. We have used coated steel; the original bones would have been whalebone.

Instructions

1. Start by stitching the bust gores as described in Chapter 3. It is best to make a quick toile to establish the

CORSET BONING

Rather than sandwiching your boning channels between the outer and lining layers of fabric, you can make up your corset unlined and use ready-made boning casing. You can use the boning casing to hide the raw edges at the centre back. Cut the front on a fold and finish it as you would with the pocket opening described in this chapter.

BUST PADS

To make bust pads, cut a long strip of wadding, roll this up and stitch over the ends and down the side to complete. Bust pads should sit under the bust and you will need to experiment with different widths and lengths of wadding to find the right size bust pads for you. When you are not using them, keep them pinned to your stays with a safety pin so as not to lose them.

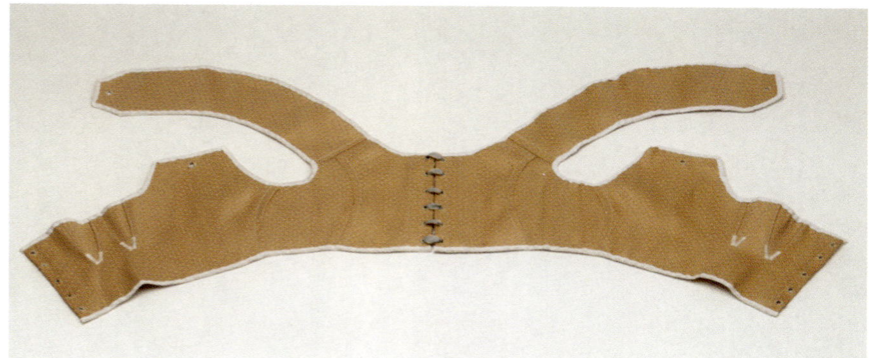

Short stays laid flat.

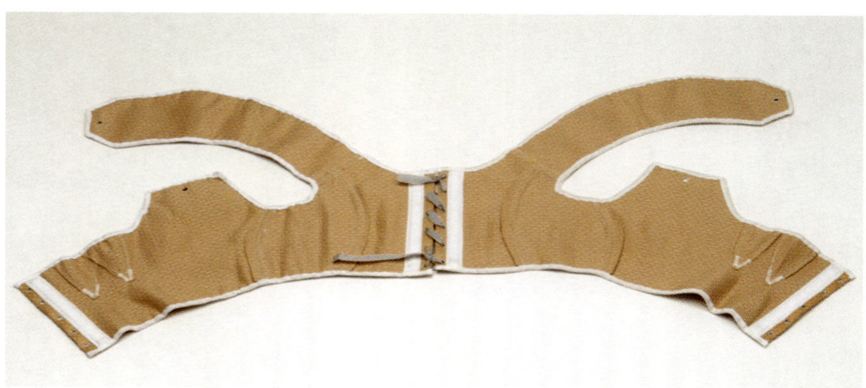

The inside of the short stays.

right place to stitch the gores for your bust size. If you have a larger bust, you may need to cut the slit lower on the stays or make the gore triangle bigger.

2. Once you have completed the gores, follow the instructions for the long stays.

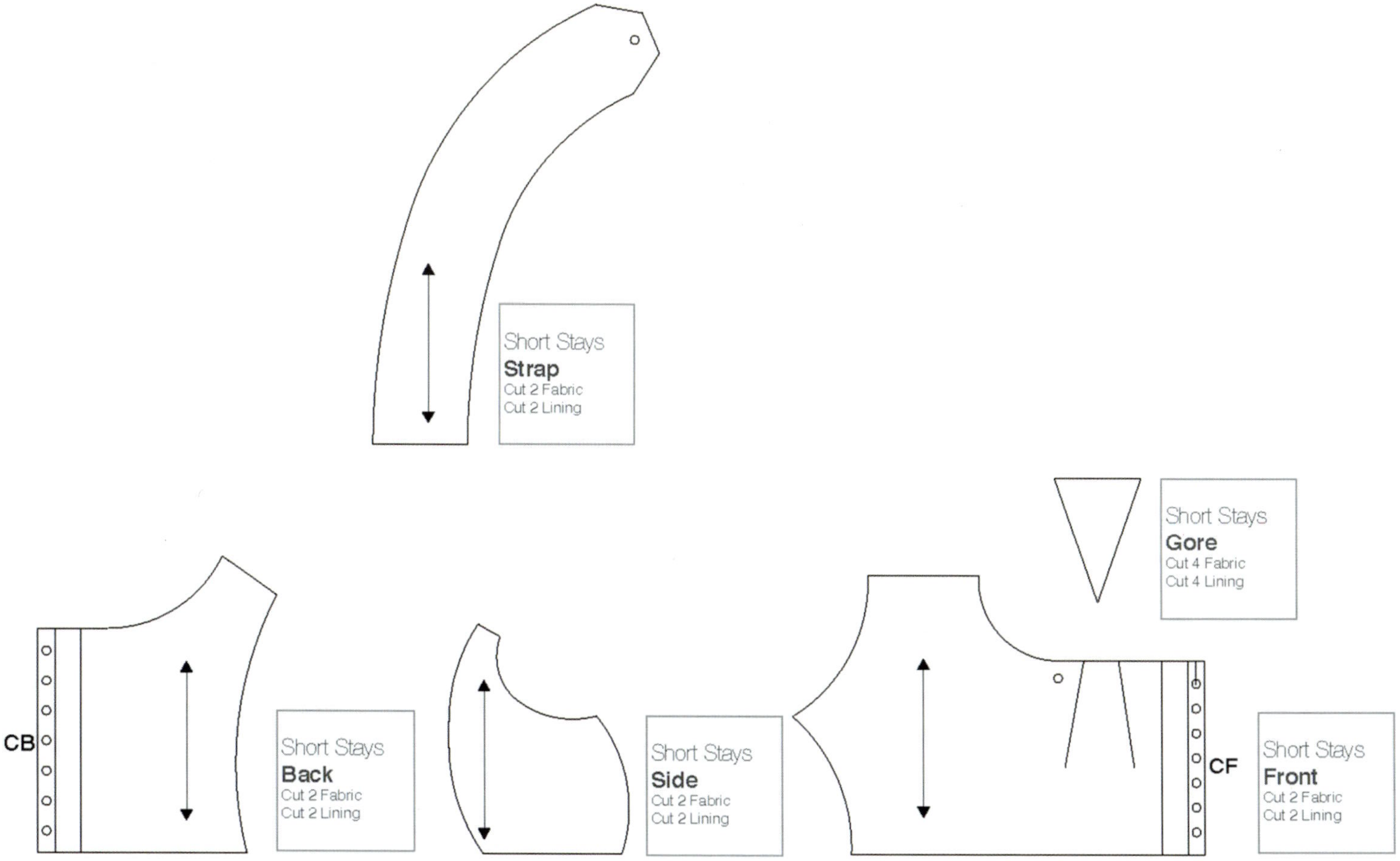

Short Stays
Strap
Cut 2 Fabric
Cut 2 Lining

Short Stays
Gore
Cut 4 Fabric
Cut 4 Lining

CB

Short Stays
Back
Cut 2 Fabric
Cut 2 Lining

Short Stays
Side
Cut 2 Fabric
Cut 2 Lining

CF

Short Stays
Front
Cut 2 Fabric
Cut 2 Lining

Short stays pattern. Scale 1:4

The petticoats shown in the book are standard and slim-width petticoats.

What You Will Need

Fabrics: For more information on how best to cut your fabric for your petticoat, see the notes on layplans below.

Other: Cord for a drawstring.

Layplans for Skirts and Petticoats

It is not her ladyship's fault that she fancies herself better than you and me. The skirts of her ancestors' garments have been kissed for centuries.

Vanity Fair, William Thackeray2

It is best to keep it simple when establishing how much fabric is needed for skirts and petticoats.

Alison in large hoop and petticoat.

Wherever possible try to use the full width of the cloth, as then you don't need to finish the edges or cut vertically into the cloth. Each length is then one panel in your skirt. How many drops or panels you need depends on how wide the fabric is and how full you wish the finished skirt to be.

The two main examples shown in this book, for either skirts or petticoats, are those with two lengths of cloth, in which the seams sit on each side of the skirt, and those with three lengths of cloth, in which two seams sit on the sides and one at the centre back, the back then being fuller than the front. Three lengths are more suitable for the early or very late skirts and two lengths are more suitable for Regency-style skirts and fuller petticoats when your fabric is very wide or heavy. Narrow petticoats can be made from one length of a reasonably wide fabric and need only one seam, which should be at the centre back.

By making your skirts or petticoats with a drawstring at the waist, you can move the fullness around to adjust how your costume looks. However, if you prefer, you can make your skirts or petticoats with a waistband by following the instructions for the riding habit skirt in Project 5.

To establish the length of material needed, measure the how long the finished skirt needs to be from your waist to where you want the skirt to finish. Then add extra for the turnings on the top and bottom of the skirt. I normally allow an extra 20cm in total. This then gives you your total panel length, which you measure down the selvage.

If you want to cut a skirt with a train, you need to add extra fabric to the panel that will sit at the back of the skirt. Then you need to curve the hem around from the front to the train measurement. It is best to do this on the stand.

When working out how much fabric you need, even if you already have enough fabric for a dress, start by working out how much you need for the skirts, then fit the smaller pieces in. If everything you need doesn't fit, you

may need to cut fewer panels in your skirt or cut one panel narrower than selvage to selvage, allowing you to fit more pieces into the fabric.

Petticoats to go over the top of the large hoops should be made up in the same manner as the skirt in Project 3. For later petticoats you can add width by cording them. Like the example shown, the simplest way to do this is to zigzag piping cord horizontally across the width of the fabric. The more authentic way of cording would be to trap the cord between two layers of fabric, stitching above and below the cord.

Instructions

1. Start by stitching the panels together and finish any raw edges.

2. Turn the top of the petticoat over twice, making sure you have enough room to thread your drawstring through the casing you have just made. Stitch through the bottom edge of the turning, catching all of the layers.

3. Make a hole by unpicking one of the vertical seams on the inside of the petticoat above the horizontal stitching completed in the last step. Then hand-stitch over the top and bottom of the hole to ensure it doesn't come undone any further.

4. Attach a safely pin to your cord and feed the cord through the casing until it comes back out. Keep the cord tied to stop it from coming out when the petticoat is not worn. If you prefer to save time when dressing, you can use elastic in the top of petticoats.

5. Mark the correct length for your petticoat, turn up the hem allowance twice and stitch.

Large Hoops

These hoops can be cut full length or shorter to save weight and fabric.

What You Will Need

Instructions

1. Stitch the hoop tops together at the centre front. Finish and press.

2. With the hoop tops right sides together, stitch along the top and sides, leaving a 2.5cm gap at the corners for the drawstring. Mitre the corners and trim down the seam allowances before turning the hoop tops the right side out. Gently push out the corners. Do this with both sides and then press.

3. Next topstitch along the top of the hoops about 2.5cm in from the top to allow room for the drawstring. Hand-stitch the raw edges at the corner gaps once you are finished

4. Stitch the sides, then hem the main hoop panels, leaving one side open. Finish and press all of the raw edges including the edges of the open panel and lay the panels flat, wrong side up.

5. Stitch the boning casing on to the panels as marked on the pattern. Leave a gap of 2.5cm in from your seam allowance and leave a flap of unstitched boning casing 2.5cm or so over each end.

6. Finish the final seam, then stitch the extra boning casing edges flat, overlapping the ends inwards, leaving enough unstitched on the top end for a final hem. These ends

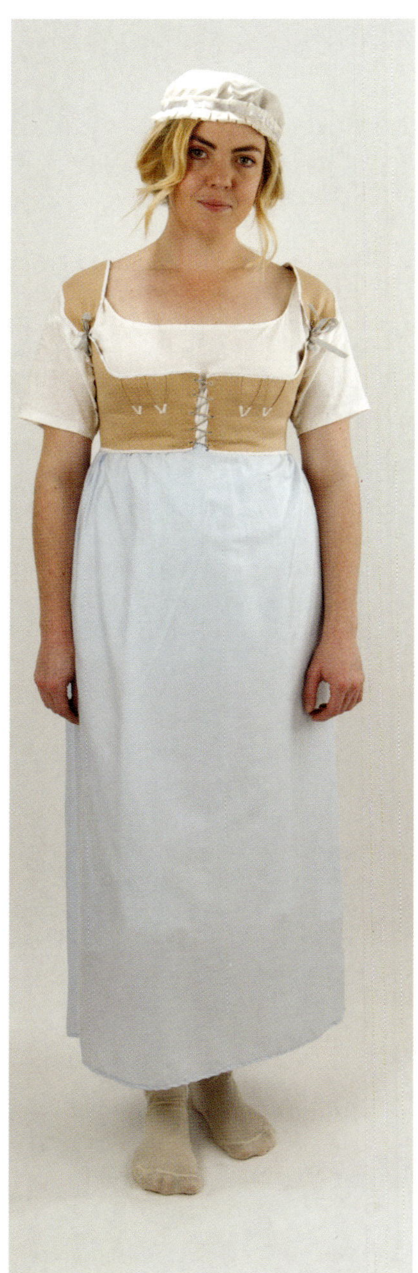

Petticoat cut from one width of fabric.

Hoop petticoat cut from three widths of fabric.

Corded petticoat cut from two widths of fabric.

Standard width petticoat cut from two widths of fabric.

should not be caught in the seam as you still need to put the boning in.

7. At the top of your hoops, attach a safely pin to your cord and feed it through the top hole until it comes out of the other side. Repeat this on the other side. Draw in to fit to your waist.

8. Next feed the boning into the boning casings, leaving about 20cm extra boning at each end. Put the hoops on the stand and play with the boning tension to work out the right shape for you. Cut off the extra boning when you are happy. Turn the last channel under and stitch it closed by hand on the inside.

Pocket Hoops

What You Will Need

Fabrics: Between 0.5 and 1 metre.

Other: Cotton cord for a drawstring, boning casing and boning. We have used coated steel, although the original would have been cane.

Instructions

1. Turn under the edge of the slits twice and stitch, tailoring the edges to the point, and overstitching the point by hand if needed. Press.

2. Turn over the top edge of the inside piece twice, stitch and press.

3. Stitch the inside square to the outside pieces along one side, finish and press.

4. Turn over the side edges of the outside piece twice and stitch. Finish the raw edges at the sides of the inside square.

5. Finish the top and the outside square, then turn down the top edge and stitch about 2.5cm down from the top to allow space for a drawstring.

6. Turn up the hem twice and stitch.

7. Lay the panels flat, wrong side up and stitch the boning casing on to the panels as marked on the pattern. Leave a gap 2.5cm in from your seam allowance and leave a flap of unstitched boning casing 2.5cm or so over each end.

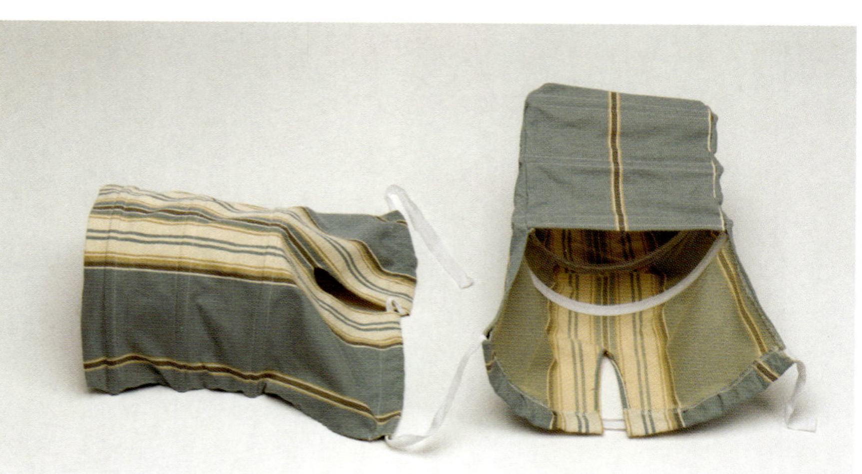

Pocket hoops.

Large hoops, shown from the front.

The front of the short hoops.

The side of the short hoops.

The back of the short hoops.

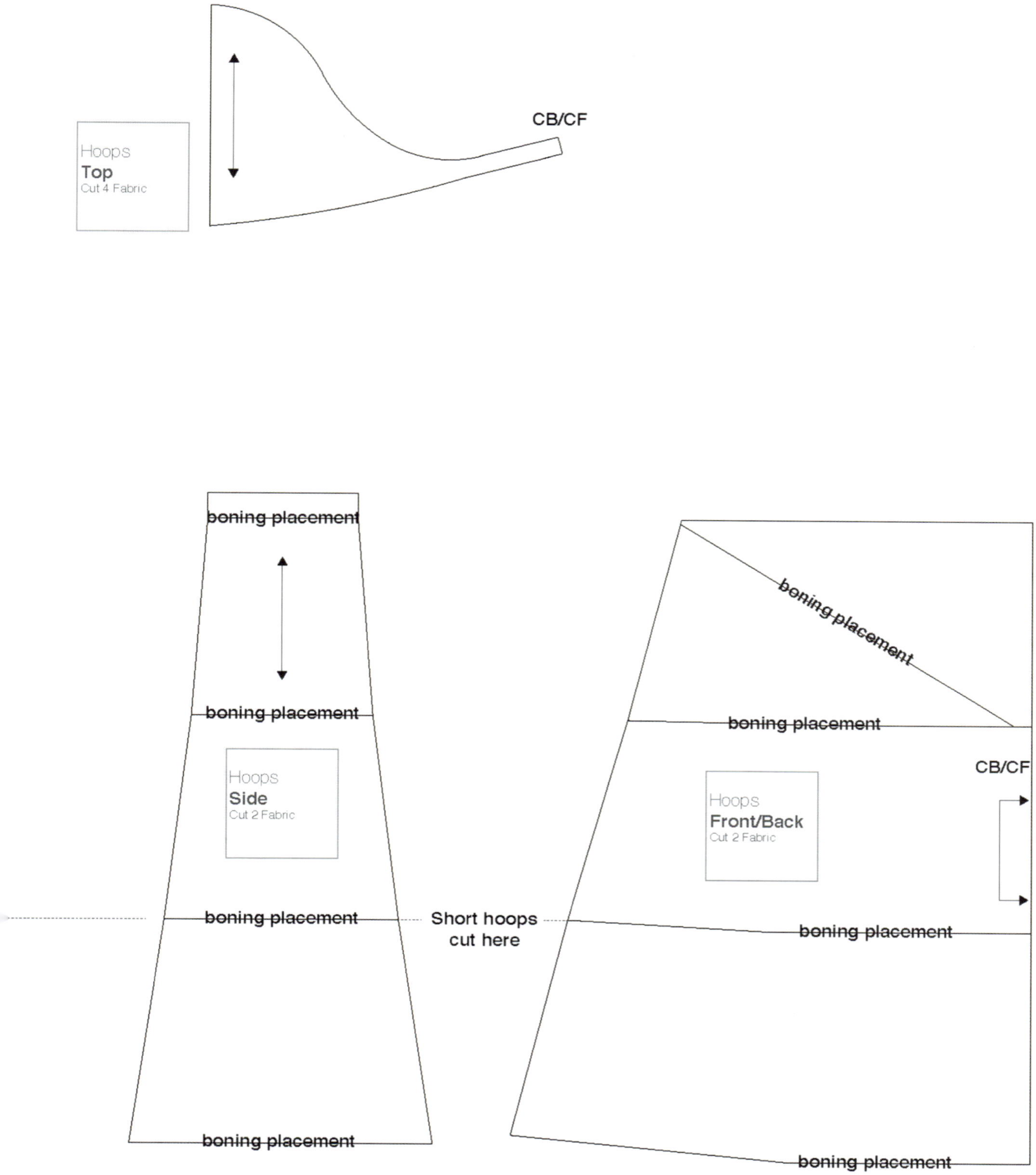

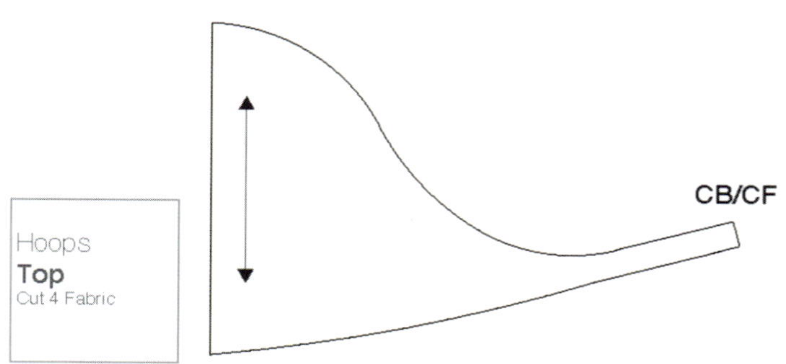

Hoop pattern. Scale 1:8

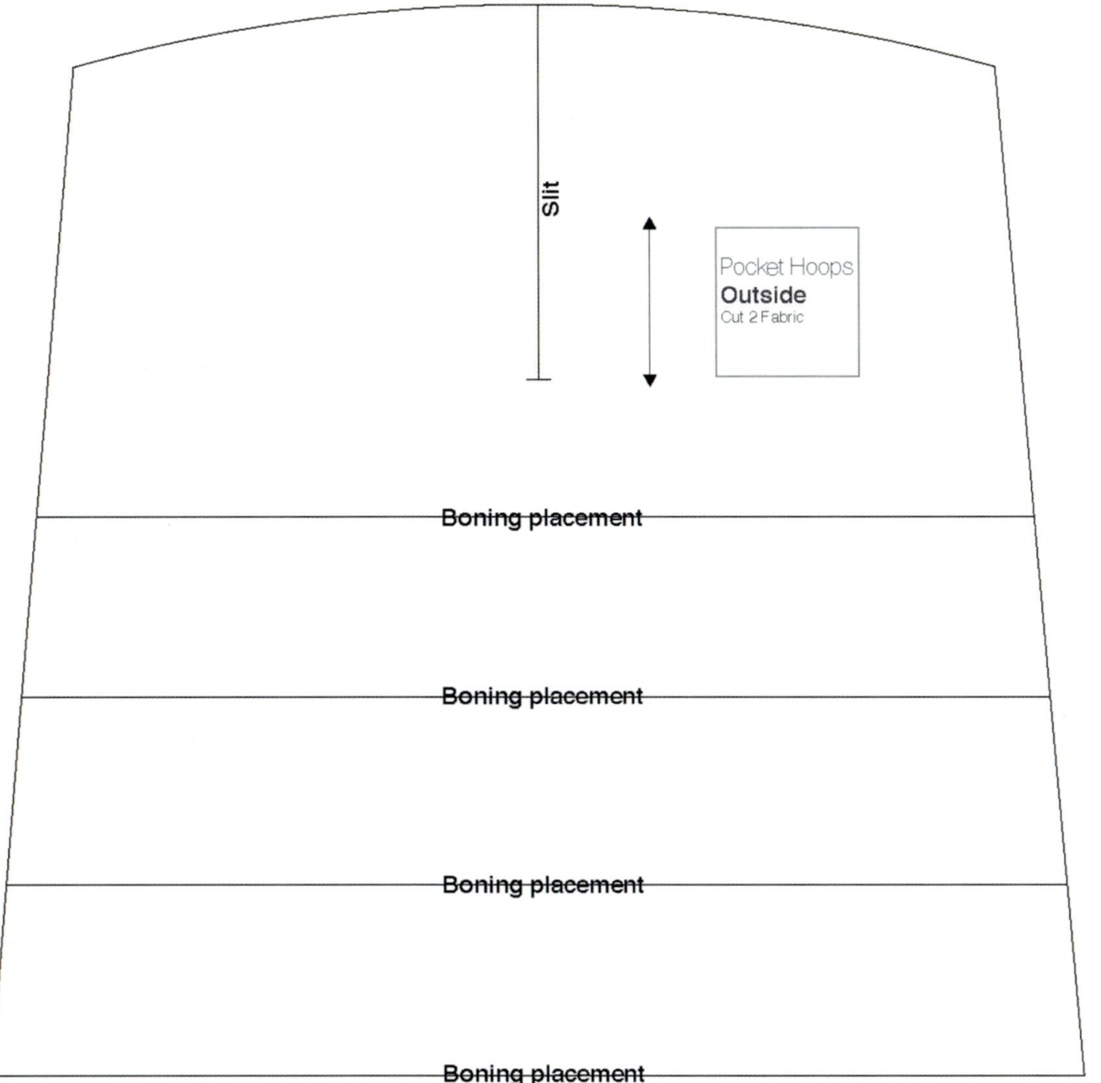

Pocket hoop pattern. Scale 1:3

8. Finish the final seam, then stitch the extra boning casing edges flat, overlapping the ends inwards, leaving enough fabric unstitched on the top end for a final hem. These ends should not be caught in the seam as you still need to put the boning in.

9. At the top of your hoops, attach a safely pin to your cord and feed it through the top hole until it comes out of the other side. Repeat this on the other side. Draw in to fit to your waist.

10. Next feed the boning into the boning casing, leaving about 20cm extra boning at each end. Put the hoops on the stand and play with the boning tension to work out the right shape for you. Cut off the extra boning and when you are happy, turn the channel under and stitch it closed by hand on the inside.

Single and Twin Pads

What You Will Need

Fabrics: Pads can be made with offcuts from other projects as you need so little fabric.

Other: Cotton cord for ties, wadding.

Instructions

1. Place pad pieces with the right sides together. Pin cotton cords in the middle of the pad and be careful not to catch them with your stitching, apart from at one end in the corners of the pad.

2. Stitch around the pad, leaving a small gap. Mitre the corners and trim down the seam allowances before turning the right side out. Gently push out the edges and press.

3. Stuff with wadding and stitch up the gap by hand to finish.

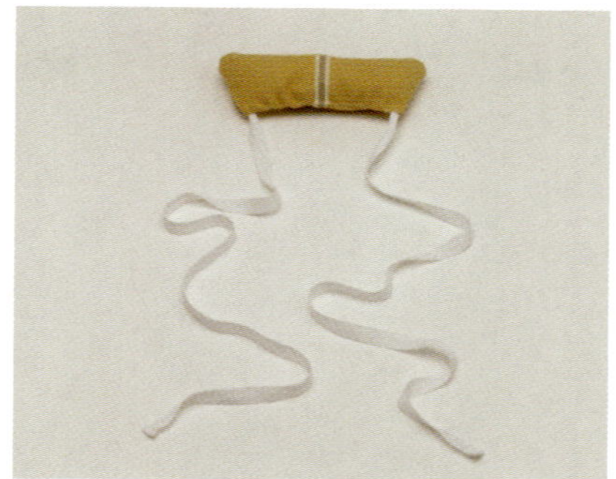

Single pad.

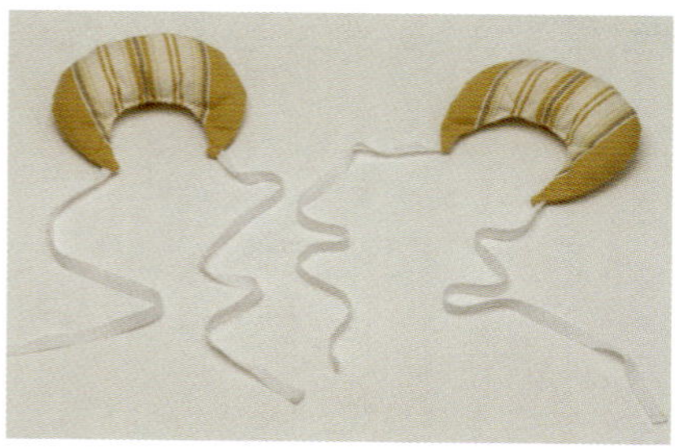

Twin pads.

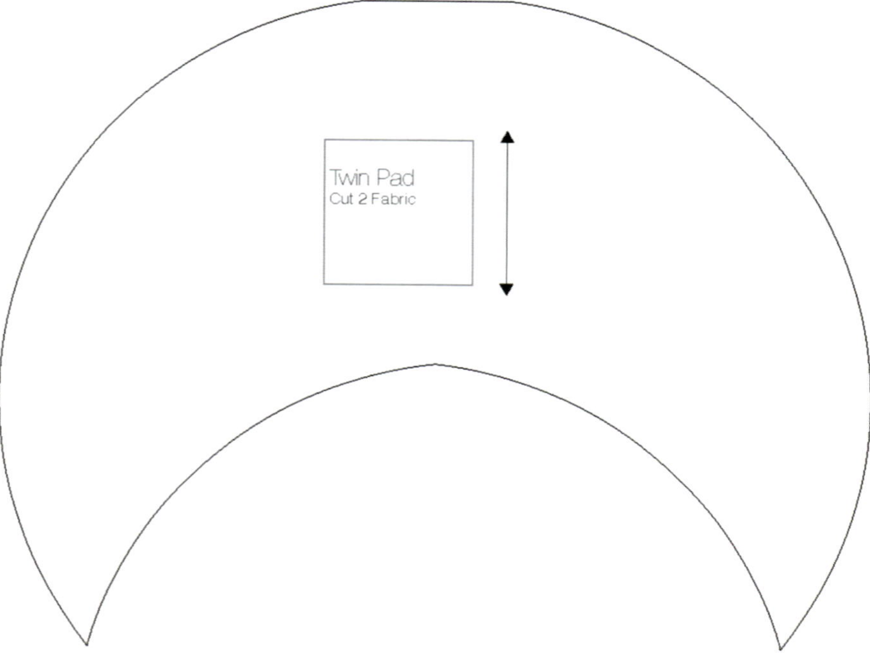

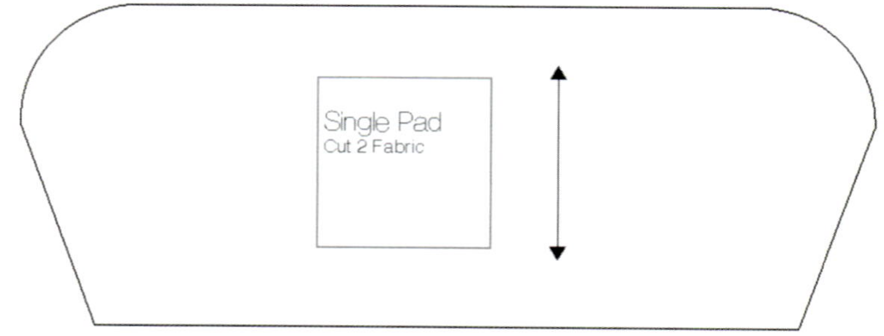

Pad pattern. Scale 1:2

In your table, as in your dress, and in all other things, I wish you to aim at propriety and neatness.

Hester Chapone3

Fontange headdress

An early eighteenth-century fashion, this headdress is worn with the early mantua in Project 1.

What You Will Need

Fabrics: About 0.5 to 1 metre of fabric, ideally a light linen, cotton or silk that has not had the gum removed from it, so it is still springy and stiff, as this stands up better when made up without a wire base.

Other: Lace trim.

Instructions

1. Start by stitching the large taps to the cap back, and then stitch the large tab lining to the taps down the side and along the bottom.

2. Mitre the corners and trim down the seam allowances. Then turn the right side out and gently push out the corners before turning the raw edge inwards and hand-stitching it down.

3. Make up the large and small frills by folding them in half and stitching them down at each end. Mitre the corners and trim down the seam allowances, before turning the right side out and gently pushing out the corners.

Back of fontange.

Side of fontange.

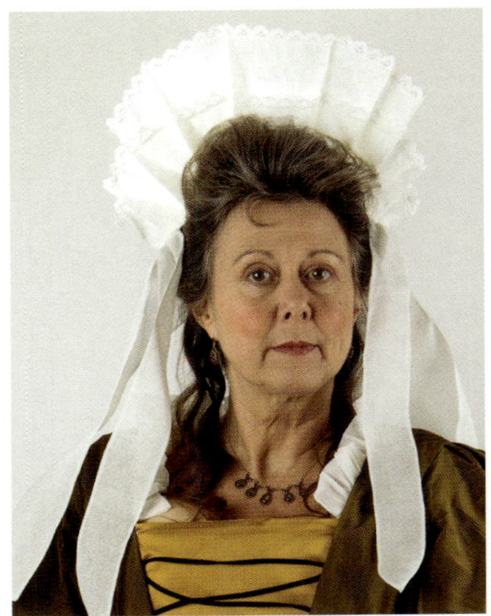

Front of fontange.

4. Stitch lace along the folded edges and press. Then gather or make pleats along the raw edge from the centre outwards, ensuring you match the centres of the frills together. Then match the frills to the headdress with the right sides together.

5. Next stitch and finish the edges before hand-stitching these flat to the inside of the headdress.

6. Finally, turn the remaining raw edge over twice and finish.

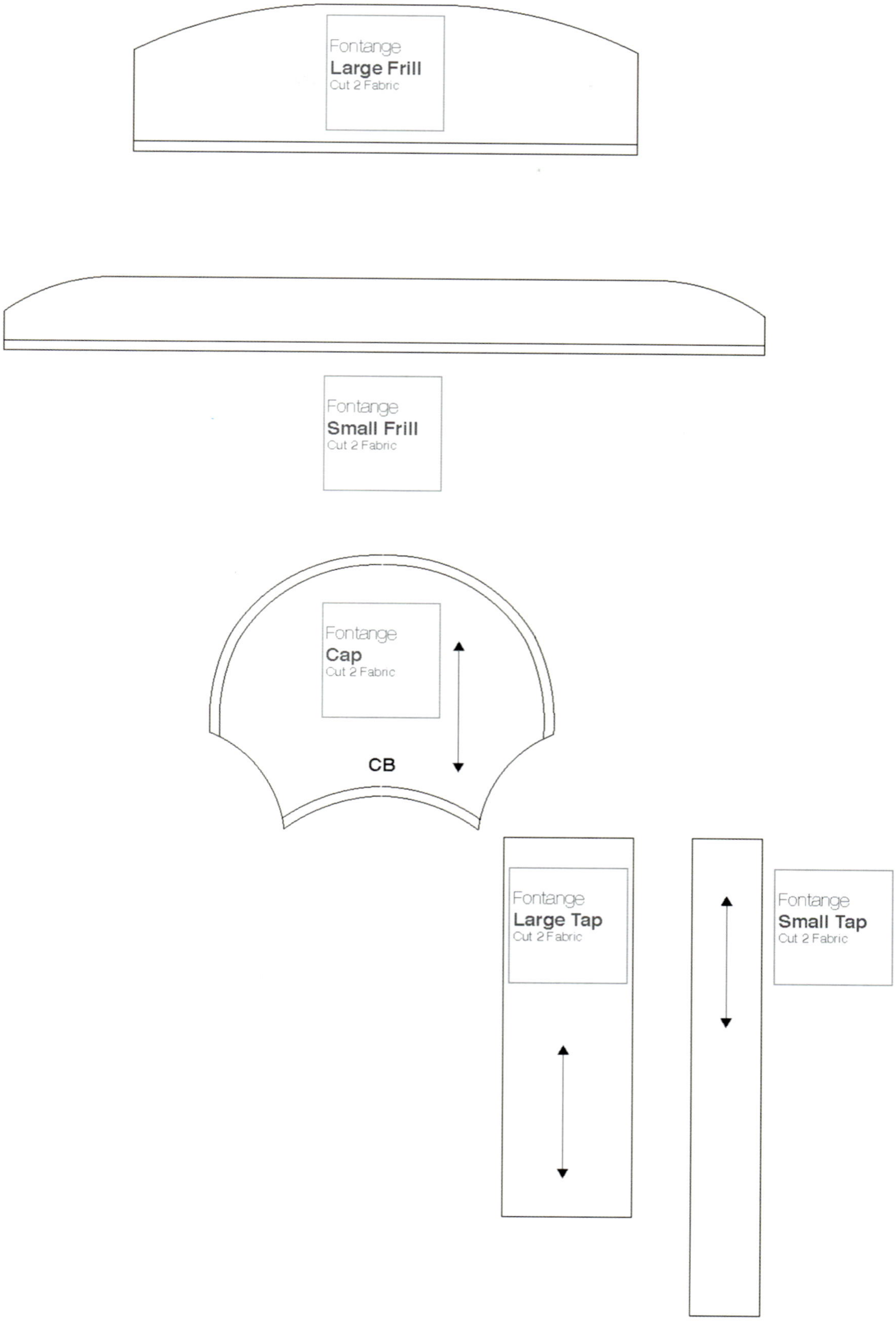

Fontange pattern. Scale 1:6

A classic Regency style, the author is shown wearing this bonnet in the introduction to this book.

What Will You Need

Fabrics: About 0.5 to 1 metre of fabric. You will also need to cut one layer in a stiff interfacing as marked on the pattern.

Other: Ribbon.

Instructions

1. Stitch seams at the centre back of all three pieces: fabric, lining and interfacing.

2. Then with the right sides together and with the interfacing on the outside, stitch around the edges.

3. Mitre the corners and trim down the seam allowances before turning the right side out and gently pushing out the edges. Press.

4. Gather as marked on the pattern and press the edges above the centre back seam inwards.

5. Pin the gathers between the back seam, press the raw edges under and stitch. Add a ribbon to finish.

Poke bonnet made from striped cotton with silk ribbons.

The underside of a poke bonnet which has been lined with the same fabric as the top side.

Poke Bonnet
Interfacing
Cut 1 Interfacing

CB

CB

Poke Bonnet
Bonnet
Cut 1 Fabric
Cut 1 Lining

CB

CB

Poke bonnet pattern. Scale 1:4

Cloak

This is a simple cloak, worn throughout the eighteenth and nineteenth centuries, which can be made into a domino as shown in Project 1.

What You Will Need

Fabrics: About 4 to 5 metres of fabric, depending on the width. It is best to adjust this pattern to suit the width of your chosen fabric, dividing the pattern up and adding more panels as needed.

Other: Hook and eye or ribbon to fasten.

Instructions

1. Piece the main cloak body pieces together, then stitch, finish and press.

2. Pleat the centre back of the hood by turning the raw edge inwards and then pinning the pleats towards the top of the hood. When you are finished, the two sides should line up with no gap, in the same way as the pleats at the side of the court dress in Project 3. Then hand-tack the pleats in place, stitch and finish the hood seam.

3. Turn under the front raw edge twice and stitch.

4. Gather or pleat the neckline between the seams so the hood fits the neck of the cape. Pin together, stitch and finish.

5. Hem the cape and add a hook and eye or ribbon at the centre front near the neck to finish.

Domino cloak.

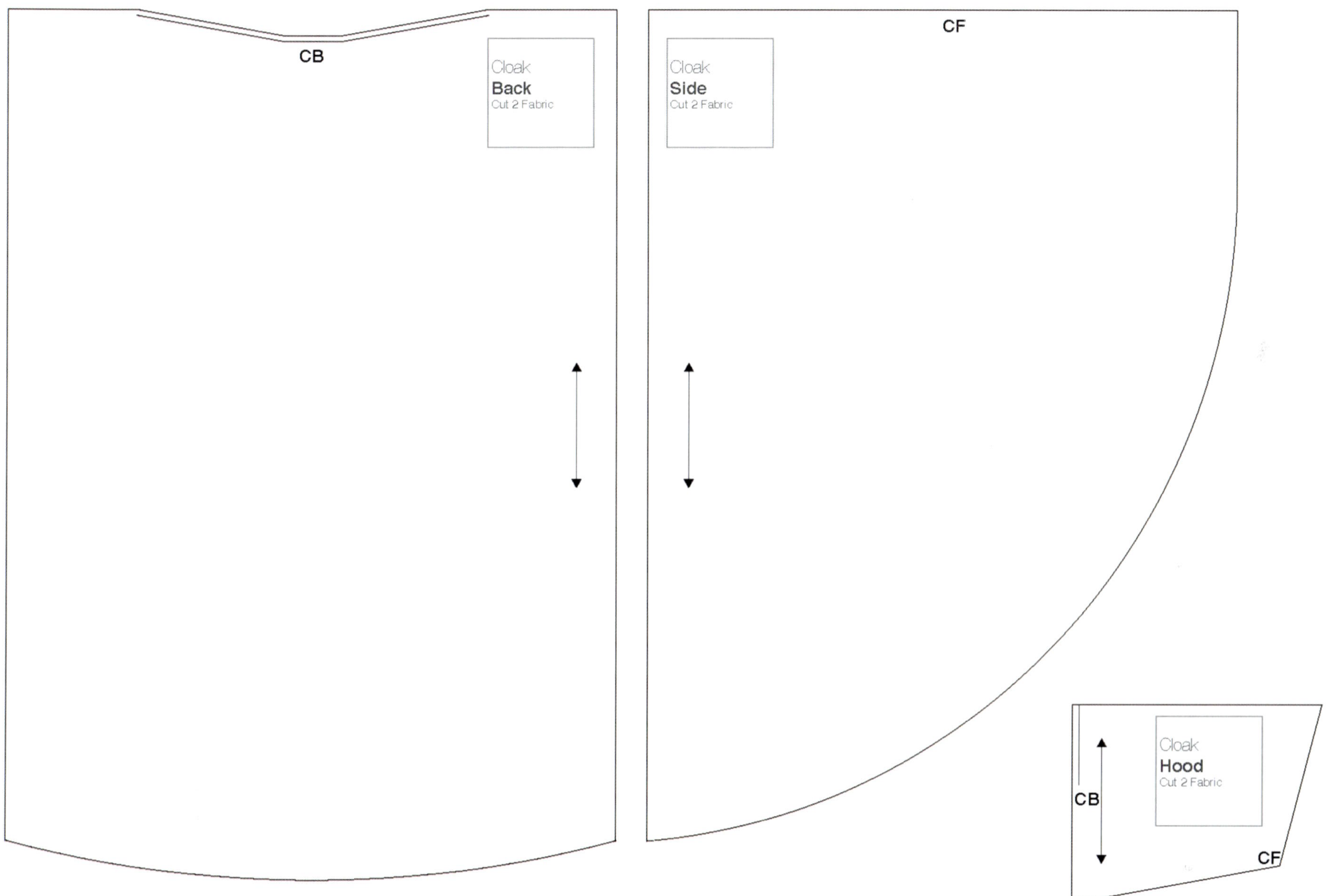

Cloak pattern. Scale 1:10

Neckerchief

These were worn by women at all levels of society throughout the eighteenth century. They were made from linen for day-to-day use and silk for special occasions.

What You Will Need

Fabrics: About a metre of fabric, as this item is cut on the bias.

Instructions

Turn over the edges of your neckerchief twice and whipstitch to complete.

A silk neckerchief.

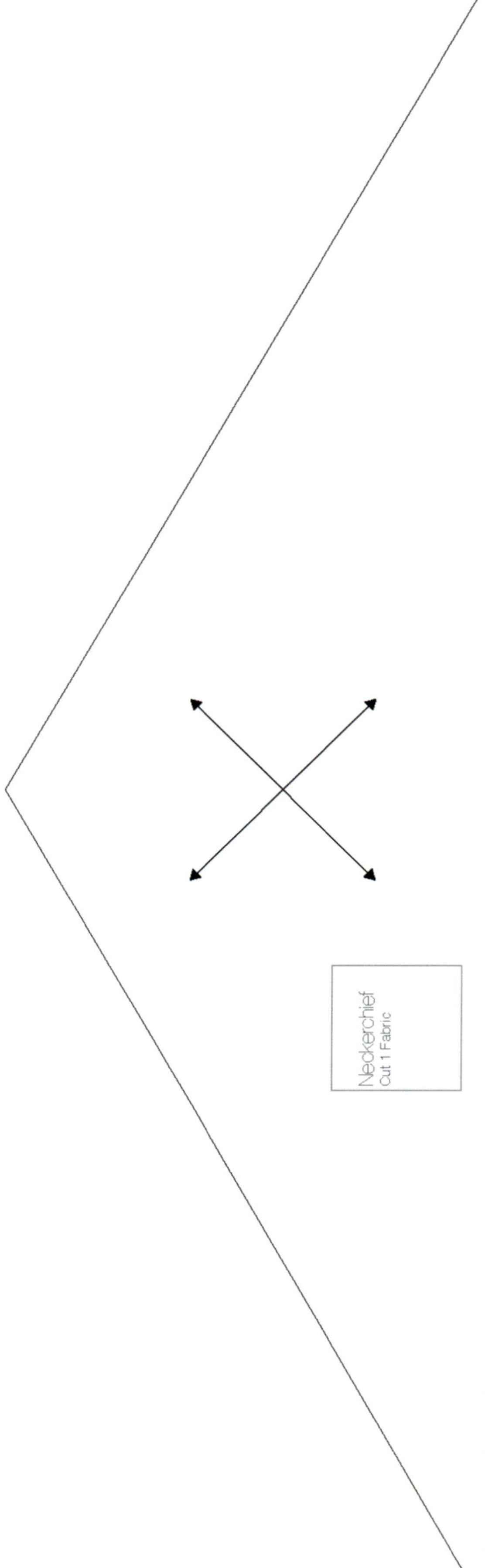

An embroidered pocket worn by Kirsten and made by Rachel Parton.

What You Will Need

Fabrics: Pockets can be made with offcuts from other projects as you need so little fabric. You can scale the pattern up or down to suit your needs.

Other: Cord for a drawstring.

Instructions

1. Turn over the edges of the slit twice and stitch, tailoring the edges to the point and overstitching the point by hand if needed. Press.

2. Put the right sides together and stitch around the edges, leaving a hole at the top edge of the top corners for the cord to thread through. Mitre the corners and trim down the seam allowances before turning the pocket the right side out and gently push out the corners.

3. Hand-stitch the raw edges in at the corners before threading the cord through the holes.

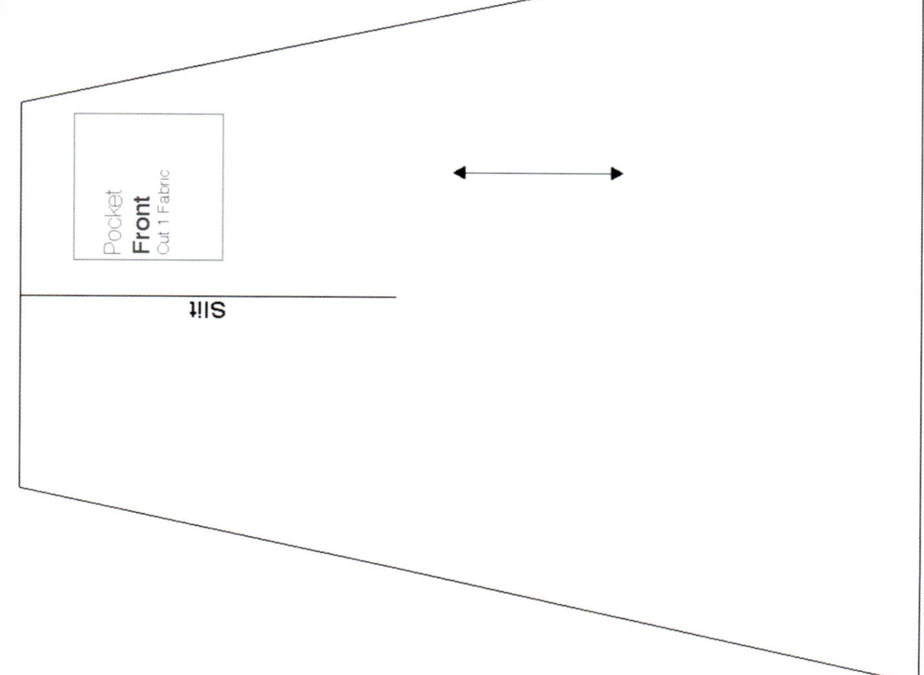

This is a simple drawstring bag, fashionable with the later slimmer fashions.

What You Will Need

Fabrics: Reticules can be made with offcuts from other projects as you need so little fabric. You could make one to match your gown.

Other: Cord or ribbon.

BEGINNERS

If you are new to costume-making, pockets or reticules are the perfect project to get you started. They are also great bases for the addition of textile decoration. See Chapter 3 and study originals for ideas.

A reticule.

Instructions

1. Put the right sides together and stitch around the edge, leaving the top open. Then trim down the seam allowances, and unless you are lining, finish.

2. Next turn the reticule the right side out and gently push out the corners.

3. Turn the top edge over twice, making sure you have enough room to thread your drawstring through the casing you have just made. Stitch through the bottom edge of the turning, catching all of the layers. Make a hole by unpicking one of the the vertical seams on the inside of the reticule above the horizontal stitching completed in the last step. Then hand-stitch over the top and bottom of the hole to ensure it doesn't come undone any further.

4. Attach a safely pin to your cord and feed the cord through the casing until it comes back out. Repeat on the opposite side and tie up or stitch both ends.

5. If you are lining your reticule, make up the lining in the same way as for the reticule and then turn the lining inside out. Finish by pressing the raw edges at the top under and hand-stitching the lining into the main bag.

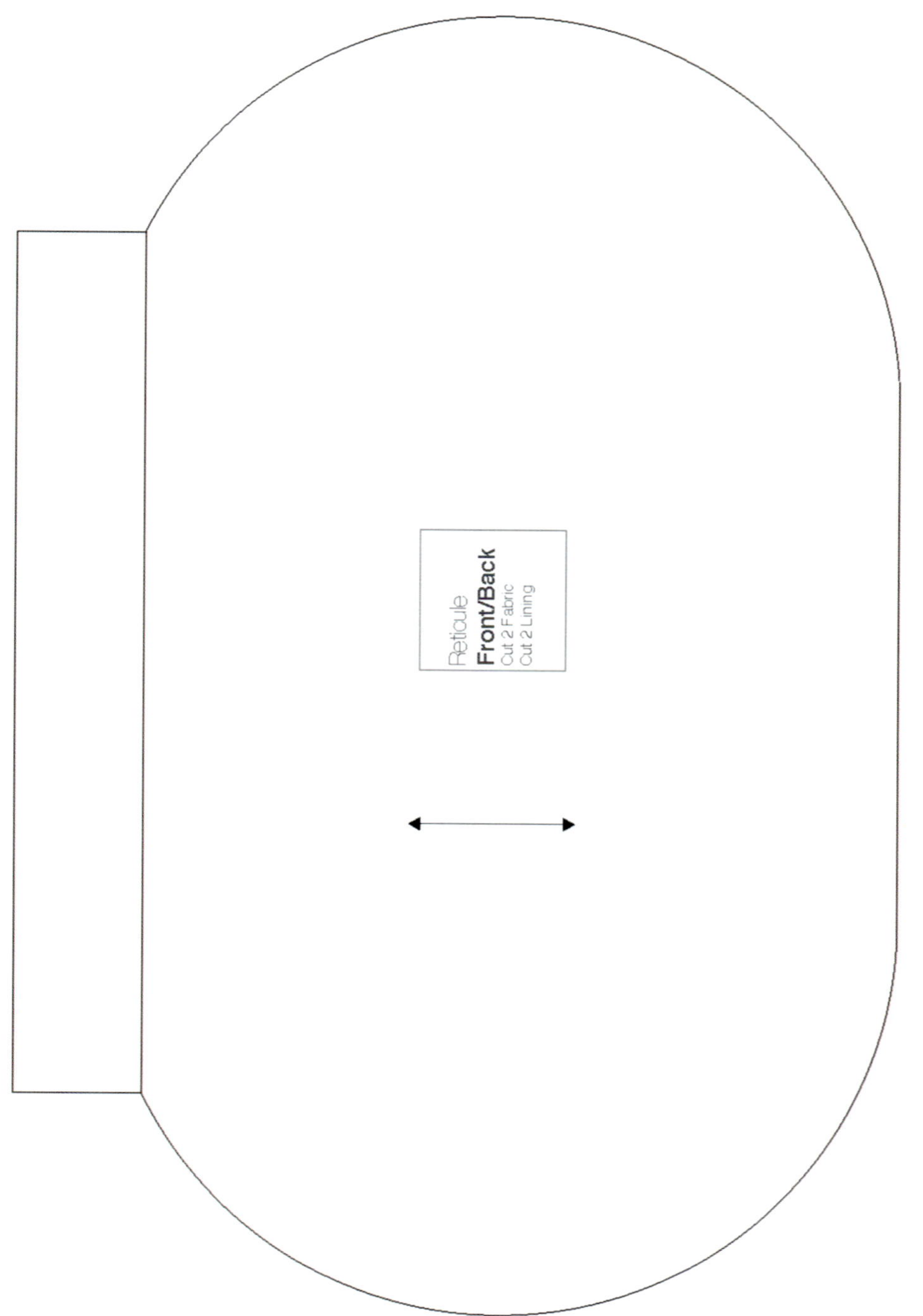

Reticule pattern. Scale 1:2

Notes

Introduction

1. Dennis Severs, 2002. *18 Folgate Street: The Tale of a House in Spitalfields*, London: Vintage.

Chapter 1

1. C. Cibber and M. Sullivan, 1973. *Colley Cibber, Three Sentimental Comedies: Love's Last Shift Or, The Fool in Fashion; The Careless Husband*, New Haven: Yale University Press.

2. E. W. Bovill, 1962. *English Country Life, 1780–1830*, Oxford: Oxford University Press.

3. F. Brawne, F. Edgcumbe and M. B. Forman, 2007. *The Letters of Fanny Brawne to Fanny Keats 1820–1824*, Whitefish: Kessinger Publishing, LLC.

4. Lady of Distinction, 2011. *The Mirror of the Graces*, Charleston: Nabu Press.

5. G. Leopardi, 2010. Dialogue Between Fashion and Death. London: Penguin Classics.

6. Lord Chesterfield, letters to his son, March 9, 1748.

7. Jeanne Louise Henriette (Genet) Campan, 2009. *Memoirs of the Court of Marie Antoinette*, The Floating Press.

8. Lady of Distinction, 2011. *The Mirror of the Graces*, Charleston: Nabu Press.

9. R. Descartes and J. Cottingham, 1986. *Rene Descartes: Meditations on First Philosophy: With Selections from the Objections and Replies* Cambridge: Cambridge University Press.

10. O. De Gouges, 2003. *Déclaration des droits de la femme et de la citoyenne; suivi de Préface pour les dames ou Le portrait des femmes.* Paris: Éd. Mille et une nuits.

Chapter 2

1. T. Steffan, E. Steffan and W. W. Pratt, 1973. *Lord Byron: Don Juan*, Harmondsworth: Penguin, 1973.

Chapter 3

1. Quoted in J. Todd and J. Todd, 1996. *Female Education in the Age of Enlightenment*, London: Pickering and Chatto (Publishers) Ltd.

2. E. Eden, 2013. *Miss Eden's Letters – The Original Classic Edition*, United States: Tebbo.

3. E. W. Bovill. and Hallett, 1962. *English Country Life, 1780–1830*, Oxford: Oxford University Press.

4. J. Penrose, J. H. Penrose and B. Mitchell, 1983. *Letters from Bath: Letters of John Penrose to His Family, 1766–67*, Gloucester: Sutton Publishing Ltd.

Chapter 4

1. Lady of Distinction, 2011. *The Mirror of the Graces*, Charleston: Nabu Press.

2. Lady of Distinction, 2011. *The Mirror of the Graces*, Charleston: Nabu Press.

3. J. Austen, 2010. *Northanger Abbey*, London: HarperPress.

Chapter 5

1. Cited in N. Jeffares, 1976. *Jonathan Swift*, Harlow: Published for the British Council by Longman Group.

2. Cited in N. Jeffares, 1976. *Jonathan Swift*, Harlow: Published for the British Council by Longman Group.

3. J. Austen, 1996. *Pride and Prejudice*, United States: Playmore Inc. Publishers.

4. C. Willett Cunnington, *The Perfect Lady.* London: Max Parrish and Co, 1948.

5. J. Austen, 1996. *Pride and Prejudice*, United States: Playmore Inc. Publishers.

6. Cited in N. Jeffares, 1976. *Jonathan Swift,* Harlow: Published for the British Council by Longman Group.

7. F. Burney, 2007. *Cecilia*, Charleston: BiblioBazaar.

8. Cited in E. W. Bovill and Hallett, 1962. *English Country Life, 1780–1830*, Oxford: Oxford University Press.

9. Mme De Remuset, cited in Jeanne Louise Henriette (Genet) Campan, 2009. *Memoirs of the Court of Marie Antoinette*, United States: The Floating Press.

10. Cited in J. Vorderstemann, 1995. *Sophie Von La Roche (1730–1807): Eine Bibliographie*, Mainz: v. Hase and Koehler.

11. J. Austen, 1996. *Pride and Prejudice*, United States: Playmore Inc. Publishers.

12. F. Burney, 1992. *Evelina: Or, the History of a Young Lady's Entrance into the World,* New York: Signet Classics.

13. J. Austen, 1996. *Pride and Prejudice,* United States: Playmore Inc. Publishers.

14. F. Burney, 1992. *Evelina: Or, the History of a Young Lady's Entrance into the World,* New York: Signet Classics.

15. F. Burney, 1992. *Evelina: Or, the History of a Young Lady's Entrance into the World,* New York: Signet Classics.

16. Cited in A. Ribeiro, 1985. *Dress in Eighteenth-century Europe, 1715–1789,* New York: Holmes and Meier Publishers Inc.

17. S. H. Beaumont, 1761. *Crito; or A dialogue on beauty,* London: R. and J. Dodsley.

18. J. Austen, 1996. *Pride and Prejudice,* United States: Playmore Inc. Publishers.

19. J. Austen, 1996. *Pride and Prejudice,* United States: Playmore Inc. Publishers.

Chapter 6

1. Cited in J. Planché, 2001. *A History of British Costume: from Ancient Times to the Eighteenth Century,* Senate.

Chapter 7

1. Cited in N. Waugh, 1994. *The Cut of Women's Clothes, 1600–1930,* New York: Routledge.

2. Cited in L. Taylor, 2002. *The Study of Dress History,* Manchester: Manchester University Press.

Chapter 8

1. W. M. Thackeray and R. Singer, 1997. *Vanity Fair,* St Louis: Turtleback Books.

Chapter 9

1. Cited in N. Waugh, 1994. *The Cut of Women's Clothes, 1600–1930,* New York: Routledge.

Chapter 10

1. Charles Otto Zieseniss *et al.,* c.1989. *The Age of Napoleon: Costume from Revolution to Empire, 1789–1815,* New York : Metropolitan Museum of Art/Harry N. Abrams.

2. *The Guardian: Nos 83–176, 16 June –1 October 1713.* 2nd edn. Manchester University Press, 2002, 1806.

3. Lady Mary Wortley Montagu and Robert Halsband. *The Complete Letters Of Lady Mary Wortley Montagu.* Oxford: Clarendon Press, 1965.

Chapter 11

1. J. Swift, 1988. *Gulliver's Travels,* Golden Books.

2. F. Burney, 1992. *Evelina: Or, the History of a Young Lady's Entrance into the World,* New York: Signet Classics.

Chapter 12

1. Cited in N. Waugh, 1994. *The Cut of Women's Clothes, 1600–1930,* New York: Routledge.

Chapter 13

1. C. Willett Cunnington, *The Perfect Lady.* London: Max Parrish and Co, 1948.

2. J. Swift, 1988. *Gulliver's Travels,* Golden Books.

Chapter 14

1. J. Austen and E. Knatchbull-Hugessen Lord Brabourne, 2009. *Letters of Jane Austen,* Vol. 2, Cambridge: Cambridge University Press.

Chapter 15

1. F. Brawne, F. Edgcumbe and M. B. Forman, 2007. *The Letters of Fanny Brawne to Fanny Keats 1820–1824,* Whitefish: Kessinger Publishing, LLC.

2. O. De Gouges, 2003. *Declaration des droits de la femme et de la citoyenne,* Paris : Mille et une nuits.

Chapter 16

1. Chapone, H. (1808) letters on the improvement of the mind, addressed to a lady.

2. *Ibid.*

3. W.M. Thackeray and R. Singer, 1997. *Vanity Fair,* St. Louis: Thackeray Books.

Suppliers

Shopping basket filled with trimmings.

The following is a list of sources of materials, covering a wide range of different prices and locations. All of those listed I have used in the past or they have been recommended to me.

Fabrics, Trimming and More

UK

www.clothhouse.com/
http://borovickfabrics.com/
www.misan.co.uk/
www.abakhan.co.uk/

www.fabricland.co.uk/
www.whitchurchsilkmill.org.uk/
www.fabricuk.com/
www.joelandsonfabrics.com/
www.liberty.co.uk/
www.macculloch-wallis.co.uk
www.historicaltextiles.com/index.html

EUROPE

www.dutchfabric.nl/sitsen/

USA and Canada

www.burnleyandtrowbridge.com
www.dharmatrading.com/
www.wmboothdraper.com/
www.puresilks.us/
http://utexsilk.com/
www.britexfabrics.com/

Australia

http://www.delectablemountain.com/
http://www.thefabricstore.com.au/

Sewing Equipment and Notions

www.morplan.com
http://www.venacavadesign.co.uk
https://www.parkinfabrics.co.uk/
http://www.kleins.co.uk/

Accessories

www.american-duchess.com
http://auldlangsynegoods.com/newHome/shoes_and_accessories.html
http://www.darcyclothing.com
http://www.austentation.com/

Suggested Reading

If you want to find out more, the following books are a good place to start and many include examples of original dress from this period.

Bradfield, N., 1995. *Costume in Details: Women's Dress, 1730–1930,* United Kingdom: Eric Dobby Publishing Ltd.

Callan, G. O., 1989. *The Encyclopaedia of Fashion: from 1840 to the 1980s,* London Thames and Hudson Ltd.

Cunnington, W. and Cunnington, P., 1992. *The History of Underclothes,* New York: Dover Publications Inc.

Fashion: The Ultimate Book of Costume and Style, 2012. London: Dorling Kindersley Publishers Ltd.

Fukai, A., Suoh, T. and Iwagami, M., 2005. *Fashion: A History from the 18th to the 20th Century,* Los Angeles: Taschen GmbH.

Hart, A. and North, S., 2000. *Historical Fashion in Detail: The 17th and 18th Centuries,* London: V & A Publications.

James, L., 1995. *Costume and Fashion: a Concise History,* London: Thames and Hudson Ltd.

Johnston, L., 2009. *Nineteenth Century Fashion in Detail,* London: Victoria and Albert Museum.

Lady of Distinction, 2011. *The Mirror of the Graces,* Charleston: Nabu Press.

MacKenzie, A., 1999. *Hats And Bonnets (Fashion and Style),* London: National Trust.

MacKenzie, A., 2004. *Embroideries (Fashion and Style),* London: National Trust.

MacKenzie, A., 2005. *Buttons And Trimmings (Fashion and Style),* London: National Trust.

Marsh, G., 2012. *18th Century Embroidery Techniques,* Lewes: Guild of Master Craftsman Publications Ltd.

Mesmer, P., 2002. *Fan Tales: from the 18th to the Beginning of the 20th Century,* United Kingdom: Parkstone Press Ltd.

Miller, L. E., 2014. *Selling Silks: A Merchant's Sample Book,* London: V & A Publishing.

Nivelon, F. and Boitard, L., 2003. *The Rudiments of Genteel Behavior: Facsimile Reprint of the First Edition of 1737,* London: Paul Holberton Publishing.

Phillips, C., 1996. *Jewellery: From Antiquity to the Present* (World of Art), London: Thames and Hudson Ltd.

Reader's Digest' *Complete Guide to Sewing, 1978.* Pleasantville: Reader's Digest Association.

Ribeiro, A., 2000. *The Gallery of Fashion,* United Kingdom: National Portrait Gallery Publications.

Steele, V., 2003. *The Corset: a Cultural History,* New Haven: Yale University Press.

Styles, J., 2010. *Threads of Feeling: the London Foundling Hospital's Textile Tokens, 1740-1770,* London: The Foundling Museum.

Georgia with a book.

Index

accessories 21, 57
aerophane 35
American War of Independence 14
Anning, Mary 15
apprentices 15
apron 21, 58

back stitch 31
balancing act 21
ballet 21
ballet dress 125–131
Baroque 14
bonnets 61, 148–149
bouillonne 35
bound seam 32
box pleats 33
burn test 39
bust gores 31
bust pads 49

cabbage 44
calculator 27
candlelight 17, 21
cape 150–151
caps 61
caraco jacket 21, 77–83
carriage dresses 21
chemise a la reine 16, 21, 109–111
circus 21
circus dress 116–117
closed robe 16
colour 18, 21
cotton 14, 15, 17, 18, 37, 38, 39
corners 33
court dress 14, 16, 21
courtiers 14
crinolines 16
cutting out 43
curves 33
Cupis de Camargo, Marie Anne de 21
Cuvrer, George 15

dancing 20, 21
day dress 21
death 20
Defoe, Daniel 14
deportment 20
directoire gown 21, 113–115
disguise 15
drawers 52

enlightenment 14
entertainment 15, 16, 21
etiquette 18–21
extinction 15
eyelet 31
eyelet punch 27

fabric 15, 17, 25, 36
fairings 65
fancy dress 73
fashion plates 21
feathers 21, 61, 65
felled seam 32
fit 45–50

flexi curve 27
flounces 34, 65
flowers 61
fontange 62, 146–147
fossils 15
Foundling Museum 18
French Revolution 14
French seam 32
full dress 21
fur 38

gathers 33
George I 15
George III 13
gloves 59
goddess 15
gowns 16
grain lines 44
grand habit 21
Grecian 16
Gulliver's Travels 14
guillotine 14

hair 16, 21, 63
handkerchiefs 13
hand stitches 31
hats 60–61
hat blocks 27
headdresses 16, 62, 146–147
Herschel, William 15
hooks and eyes/loops 27
hoops 16, 21, 53

informal (dress) 20
iron/ironing board 27

Jenner, Edward 14
jewellery 63–64
jewels 65

knife pleats 33

lace 61
Laennec, Rene 15
Lavisier, Antoine 15
laws 15
leather 32, 39
leather punch 27
linen 38
lining 32
Louis XV 16
Louis XVI 14

make up 63
manners 18–21
mannequin 27
mantua 14, 16, 21, 67–73
masking tape 27
masquerade 15
maternity 21
measures 27
medicine 14
morning dress 20
mourning dress 25
mitts 59
muffs 59

Napoleon 14
Napoleonic wars 14
neckerchief 58, 152
needles, sewing 21
neoclassical 14
notches 44
novel 14

open robe 16
overcast seam 32
oxygen 15

pads dress 16, 145
painted decoration textile 35
panniers 14, 16, 53, 141–144
parasol 59
pattern alteration 41
pattern fabric 45
pattern fit 41
pattern markings 67
pattern paper 27
patterns scaling up 41
pauper 15, 16, 56
pencils 27
petticoats 52
pins 27, 65
pin cushion 27
pin tucks 33
pinking 34
pleats 33
pockets 57, 153
pocket hoops 141–144
poke bonnet 17, 148–149
pompon 59
poppers 27
posture 20
Priestley, Joseph 15
prints fabric 17, 44
promenade dresses 21
pregnancy 21, 75

quilting 35
Queen Anne 13
Queen Victoria 13

redicule 58, 154–155
reducing bulk 33
Regency gown 21, 199–123
Regency gown, late 21, 125–131
ribbons 13, 17, 65
riding habit 16, 21, 99–103
Robinson Crusoe 14
Rococo 14
robe a langlaise 16, 21, 105–107
robe a la francaise 14, 21, 91 -95
robe a la polonaise 16, 21, 105–107
robe de cour 21, 85–89
robe volante 16, 21, 75–80
Romantic Movement 16
rope walker 21
Rouleau loop turner 27
ruffles 34, 61
running stitch 31

sack back 16, 48
safety pins 27

scandal 20
scissors 27
seaside dresses 21
seams 32
seam allowance 43
Settlement Act 15
sequins 35
sewing machine 27
shawls 58
shepherdess 15
shift 51, 133–134
shoes 60
silks 14, 18, 37, 39
silk worms 18
skin 38
skirts, fitting, 47
skirts, patterns 139
sleeves, fitting 46
slip stitch 31
smallpox 14–15
snaps 27
Spencer jacket 17, 119–123
sport 16
stitch unpick 27
stays 52, 135–136, 137–138
stethoscope 15
stockings 51
stomacher 21
stripes 45
Sumptuary Laws 15
Swift, Jonathan 14

thieves 18
Taglioni 21
tailored 17
tails 67, 70
thimble 27
thread 27
toile 45–50
tippets 61
train, dress 21, 69
travelling costume 21
Treaty of Paris 14
trims/trimmings 15, 65
tucks 33
turbans 62
turned and stitched seams 32

underpinnings/undergarments 16, 17, 51
undress 20–21

vaccine 14

weavers 18
waistcoat 21
walking 20
walking dress 21
weddings 21
weights 27
whip stitch 31
wigs 16, 63
wills 17
wool/woollen cloth 17, 38
workspace 27
woven fabrics 37

"